The East Coast Main Line
King's Cross to Edinburgh

*MARTIN BUCK*

*&*

*MARK RAWLINSON*

*Freightmaster*
*Publishing*

# CONTENTS

INTRODUCTION. . . . . . . . . . . . . . . . . . . . . . . . . . . . . . . . . . . . .   3

OVERVIEW . . . . . . . . . . . . . . . . . . . . . . . . . . . . . . . . . . . . . . .   4

LEGEND . . . . . . . . . . . . . . . . . . . . . . . . . . . . . . . . . . . . . . . . .   8

KING'S CROSS to BERWICK-upon-TWEED . . . . . . . . . . . . . . . . . . . . .   9

GALLERY. . . . . . . . . . . . . . . . . . . . . . . . . . . . . . . . . . . . . . . . .  89

BERWICK-upon-TWEED to CARSTAIRS . . . . . . . . . . . . . . . . . . . . . . . 105

HERTFORD LOOP. . . . . . . . . . . . . . . . . . . . . . . . . . . . . . . . . . . 129

GLOSSARY :      Miles & Chains . . . . . . . . . . . . . . . . . . . . . . . . . . . 136
                Acknowledgements . . . . . . . . . . . . . . . . . . . . . . . . . 140
                Photographers. . . . . . . . . . . . . . . . . . . . . . . . . . . . 140
                Bibliography . . . . . . . . . . . . . . . . . . . . . . . . . . . . . 140

Schematic Maps & Research    :    Mark Rawlinson
                     e-mail    :    mark.rawlinson@virgin.net
                        fax    :    01524-730591

Layout, Text & Captions    :    Martin Buck
                 e-mail    :    martin.buck1@virgin.net
                    fax    :    01793-644079

                   ISBN    :    0-9537540-2-2

           Published by    :    Freightmaster Publishing
                                158 Overbrook
                                SWINDON SN3 6AY

             Printed by    :    Tekprint Ltd., SWINDON

Front Cover Designed by    :    Tekprint Ltd.

# INTRODUCTION

**THANK YOU** for buying this copy of LINE BY LINE, the third book in our series of fully illustrated guides on famous railway routes.

This volume features the East Coast Main Line and should have been the second publication in this series, but the Great Western Main Line took precedence due to customer demand - apologies to those who have waited patiently for this one!

**THIS EDITION** covers the East Coast route to Scotland from London King's Cross to Edinburgh Waverley, which we have extended to Carstairs as GNER (Great North Eastern Railway) operate direct services to Glasgow Central. The route between the latter two locations can be traced in the first LINE BY LINE : the West Coast Main Line.

Additionally, the line between Alexandra Palace and Langley Junction (just south of Stevenage) via Hertford North, the 'Hertford Loop', is also featured.

**EVERY PAGE** you turn will reveal a ten-mile, schematic, cross section of the route spread across two pages showing the gradient profile & topography, track plan and station layouts along with two recent photographs to illustrate a location of interest.

Periodically, this sequence is broken with several pages of more than one photograph to illustrate additional locations. The photographs also provide representative coverage of both the motive power and rolling stock associated with the East Coast Main Line around the turn of the second Millennium.

As far as gradient profiles are concerned, this book exclusively illustrates the gradient profile for the Penmanshiel diversion, which came into effect in 1979 following the Penmanshiel Tunnel collapse, and the Selby diversion, which opened in 1983 between Temple Hirst Junction and Colton Junction.

We start at King's Cross station, from where the route is traced northwards in 5-mile sections until our journey is completed over 400 miles and 140 pages later.

**A 'GALLERY'** section includes high calibre colour photographs of some classic locations on the northern stretch of the ECML where the line skirts the North Sea around Berwick-upon-Tweed and passes the Lammermuir Hills near Penmanshiel. Full-colour reproductions of Ordnance Survey Landranger maps are also included to show the location of each view.

**FINALLY** we would like to extend our thanks to the Ordnance Survey for allowing us to reproduce their Landranger maps along with those people named in the Glossary, who have kindly contributed photographs for inclusion in this volume.

# OVERVIEW

## *Background:*

The East Coast Main Line (ECML) is considered by many to be the most prestigious main line on the railway network and it carries Britain's fastest passenger train service, while also handling heavy bulk freight and mail trains.

GNER has the responsibility of running inter-city passenger services, mainly using a fleet of Class 91 electric locomotives and Mark.4 coaches. These 'electric' services run to Edinburgh Waverley and through workings to towns and cities off the electrified main line, such as Aberdeen, is the preserve of High Speed Train sets (HST).

When thinking about the ECML, two famous trains readily spring to mind. The "Flying Scotsman", synonymous over the years with the ten o'clock departure from King's Cross to Edinburgh and the name of probably the most well known steam locomotive in the world, an A3 pacific with a 4-6-2 wheel arrangement, designed by Sir Nigel Gresley.

The "Elizabethan", affectionately known as the "non-stop", ran in both directions between King's Cross and Edinburgh with no intermediate stops. This train was hauled by an A4 pacific, but coupled behind the engine was the device that made the "non-stop" possible - a corridor coal tender, which enabled two sets of train crew to changeover en-route. At the time, this journey was the longest non-stop passenger train service in the world. The last non-stop runs finished on 9th September 1961 and now all trains call at York and Newcastle.

The ECML has long been associated with fast running and trains of special interest. For example, the streamlined pacific Mallard achieved 126mph on 3rd July, 1938, in the course of brake tests, which has remained the all-time record for steam traction.

Then there were the 'named' trains, formed of distinctive 'chocolate & cream' Pullman cars, such as the Tyne-Tees Pullman and, above all, the famous Queen of Scots Pullman. Sadly, by the 1970s, the remaining Pullman cars had been re-liveried into British Rail grey & blue and by June 1978 these eye-catching trains had disappeared from the ECML altogether. To-day, some of these famous names live on, albeit in name only for a handful of Class 91/HST scheduled passenger services.

Two types of locomotive have had long associations with the ECML, which captured the imagination of the railway fraternity - the Gresley pacific steam locomotives and the 'Deltic' diesel locomotive, the latter being withdrawn from passenger service in December 1981, having gained cult status among railway enthusiasts.

## Historical Perspective:

GNER secured a seven year franchise from InterCity to operate high-speed passenger services on the ECML following the privatisation of British Rail, which in turn emerged from the nationalisation of the London & North Eastern Railway (LNER) in 1948. GNER commenced operating in April 1996 although the historical roots of this great line stretch back much further in time.

It can be said that the LNER had its roots with George Stephenson and the world's first public railway. The largest, most wealthy and influential constituent company - the North Eastern - evolved from the Stockton & Darlington, which opened in 1825. The North Eastern had a virtual monopoly in the North and Yorkshire, Durham and Northumberland, including running powers through North British territory to Edinburgh.

The next largest company was the Great Northern bordering and south of the North Eastern; the two lines with the help of the North British over the border, formed the East Coast route to Scotland. The Great Northern did not come into being until 1846 and from the start it set Yorkshire as its base; King's Cross was its London terminus from 1852. In Scotland, the LNER absorbed the North British.

The first trains to reach York from London did so via Rugby using the York & North Midland Railway and by 1844 there was a through service from the Thames to the Tyne via Darlington, Penshaw, Washington and Boldon. In 1846 the North British Railway opened from Edinburgh to Berwick followed in 1847 by Berwick to Newcastle - both links completed by the High Level Bridge at Newcastle and the Royal Border Bridge spanning the River Tweed at Berwick; both products of Robert Stephenson.

The direct route between London and York was completed in 1852. The main lines from Doncaster to York through Selby (prior to the 'Selby Diversion') and from Ferryhill to Durham did not come into use until 1872.

The last links to be inserted to make up the current route of the ECML were constructed more than 75 years apart. The King Edward Bridge across the River Tyne in Newcastle was opened in 1906, before which all trains had to use the High Level Bridge and reverse in Newcastle station.

Finally, the 'Selby Diversion' opened to passenger traffic in 1983 between Temple Hirst Junction and Colton Junction, which was constructed (with heavy National Coal Board subsidy) due to mining subsidence at the Selby coalfield. This new line also removed a bottleneck where the old line crossed the River Ouse at Selby by means of a swing bridge.

## Modernisation: Signalling & Electrification

Resignalling and electrification are by far the two most important engineering projects which have helped to make the ECML a modern day high-speed route.

It is probably true that much of the country on the southern half of the ECML is flat, affording little of interest from the carriage window. From the outset, this factor has enabled the engineers to construct a railway with a bias towards speed - in particular, the stretch between York and Darlington, virtually straight and level for some 44 miles, has always been known as the "Racing Grounds."

North of Darlington the line becomes more sinuous as it crosses numerous river valleys in Durham and Northumberland, involving major engineering features and sharp curves - the most notable curve being at Morpeth. From here, the ECML really is on the East Coast and fast running once again resumes. The only gradient of note on the entire route is encountered near the Lammermuir Hills, where southbound trains face a severe incline stretching 4½ miles at a 1 in 96 gradient to Grantshouse.

In 1948, the year when the railways in Britain were nationalised, there were 286 signal boxes to control traffic on the ECML between King's Cross and Edinburgh Waverley. During the 1950s, new power signalboxes were commissioned at York and Newcastle and following the 1955 Modernisation Plan, unlike the WCML, re-signalling of the ECML was a protracted and piecemeal affair, which was only completed 2½ years before the Government gave the approval for full electrification in 1984.

Until the late 1970s, trains in many areas of the ECML were still controlled with oil-lit semaphore signals operated from pre-grouping mechanical signalboxes. In 1969 the shell of a new Power Signal Box (PSB) was started at King's Cross and by the end of 1970, approval was given to re-signal the line between London and Sandy. A year later, the go ahead was given for electrification of suburban services to Royston via Hitchin and Hertford North.

At the beginning of 1972, approval was given for a new PSB at Peterborough along with the remodelling of tracks - the layout at Peterborough station was so bad that all trains were restricted to 20mph. By May 1973 this work had been completed and trains could pass through the area at 100mph!

In 1974, GEC secured the contract to provide Multiple Aspect Signalling (MAS) between Sandy and Holme and between Helpston and Stoke Tunnel, thus extending the area controlled by the Peterborough panel. Authorisation was also given for a new PSB at Doncaster, with the contract being awarded to the world-famous Westinghouse Brake & Signal Company in 1975.

In 1977, King's Cross PSB was finally commissioned, controlling 83½ route miles, and work started to remodel and simplify the track layout at the station's throat. Overhead wires appeared for the first time and from 3rd October 1977, the first suburban electric services started running.

The last semaphore disappeared from the ECML on 27th September 1978, when the up home at Doncaster decoy No. 2 was removed and Doncaster PSB was finally fully commissioned in December 1981. This commissioning was planned for three years previous, to coincide with the introduction of the Eastern Region's new fleet of HSTs. In Scotland, a new PSB at Edinburgh Waverley was commissioned and in March 1978, MAS was brought into use between Edinburgh and Berwick.

In 1988, work started on a new Integrated Electronic Control Centre (IECC), a more up-to-date power signalbox, at York as part of the ECML electrification project. This new type of signalling centre dispensed with the illuminated track diagram 'panels', replaced by signalmen's workstations equipped with VDUs and keyboards! The IECC was fully commissioned in April 1990 when resignalling north of York had been completed, resulting in Tollerton, Thirsk and Northallerton signalboxes being closed.

Work continued northwards and a second IECC was built at Newcastle on the south bank of the River Tyne and this controlled the lines from Darlington through to Morpeth. The signalboxes at both Alnmouth and Tweedmouth were retained due to the high number of CCTV-controlled level crossings on the route north of Morpeth.

When resignalling was complete, the ECML between London and Edinburgh was controlled from just nine signalling centres at Kings' Cross, Peterborough, Doncaster, York, Newcastle, Morpeth, Alnmouth, Tweedmouth and Edinburgh. Furthermore, most of the ECML north of York was signalled for bi-directional running.

The electrification project involved an extensive civil engineering programme which involved 157 bridges being raised or rebuilt, tracks slewed or lowered, and nine station layouts simplified. Major track rationalisation took place at York, where the through lines at the station were removed and the famous diamond crossings at the north end of Newcastle station were replaced by simple turnouts.

Some architectural structures were of such historical importance that special considerations had to be made. To preserve the structure of Durham viaduct for the future, the deck was waterproofed by laying an impervious membrane, on which a concrete surface was laid prior to ballasting. Here, and at the Royal Border Bridge at Berwick, the thought of the obtrusive, standard design, overhead catenary crossing these viaducts was considered inappropriate. A firm of engineering consultants, Ove Arup, remedied the situation by designing slimmer catenary equipment to cross them both.

To cater for electrification at Morpeth, a station situated on a tight curve, the decorative awning had to be moved back from the platform edge by over 3ft. This was achieved by jacks raising the support columns, slides inserted beneath them, followed by hydraulic rams pushing the entire awning into its new position - thus saving another 'listed' structure!

In Scotland, one major operation was the singling and relining of the south bore of Calton Tunnel, just outside Edinbugh Waverley station. The tunnel was a bare rock tunnel and the inside condition was not suitable for either raising the roof or lowering the floor. The answer was to single the track and to ensure the tunnel lasted well into the next century, some dramatic work was carried out inside it. Circular lining sections were bolted together and fixed to the rock with some 1,000 rock bolts, with the space between the linings and the original walls filled with grout.

In comparison, a smaller project saw the old footbridge at Drem station replaced by a new fabricated one, which combined modern design with the traditional. Many other bridges also needed to be raised or replaced, including the big footbridge across the west end of Waverley station.

At the time, British Rail was keen to raise public awareness of the electrification project and staged many ceremonies, which made the local or national newspapers or television networks. For example, the first Class 91 locomotive was named Swallow at King's Cross, attended by Sir Robert Reid (Chairman of British rail) and Lord Prior (Chairman of GEC). On a less grandiose scale, a 'mast-planting' ceremony was held to mark the 10,000th electrification mast planted at Grantham on 15th October 1986!

Construction of the overhead network was centred on depots at Peterborough, Doncaster, Newcastle and Edinburgh (Millerhill) and when electrification had been completed, management of the system was controlled from offices at just three centres: Hornsey, Doncaster and Cathcart.

From a motive power perspective, the electrification project, like that of the WCML, gave rise to a whole new class of locomotive and rolling stock to haul the new electric services. These new train sets would ultimately be made up of a Class 91 + 9 Mark 4 coaches + a Class 82 Driving Van Trailer (DVT); the latter being a novel concept enabling the train to be driven from either end, first introduced on the WCML in 1988.

From May 1989, a number of diagrams featured a Class 91 locomotive hauling Mark 3 coaches plus DVT and in October 1989 the first Mark 4 coaches entered service on the 'Yorkshire Pullman' between Leeds and King's Cross. The new trains were phased in to service to coincide with the progress of electrification and it was not until May 1991 when through electric services reached Edinburgh Waverley.

## *The Future:*

A recent review established that the ECML is operating at near capacity and with passenger and freight operators wishing to run more trains and reduce journey times, it was clear that the present infrastructure would not be able to cope. The ECML has a large number of 'bottlenecks' throughout its length, where sections of line, stations and junctions can barely cope with present timetables. These 'bottlenecks' give little leeway to deal with late running services or incidents.

As a result, an upgrade of the ECML was proposed, taking in 4 phases, the last of which being due for completion by 2010 and all having some very interesting engineering challenges.

Phase 1 is well underway with some notable ahievements to date. An £8 million replacement of Newark Dyke Bridge over the River Trent was completed in August 2000, resulting in trains being able to cross it at a speed of 125mph. A further £4 million spend saw the remodelling of Doncaster South Yorkshire Junction which increased capacity and alleviated congestion at a major 'bottleneck'.

Phase 2 includes extra platforms at King's Cross and Peterborough station; Phase 3, the construction of 'flyovers' at Hitchin, Newark and Doncaster and Phase 4 involves removing the current two track bottleneck at Welwyn by the construction of a new viaduct and two new tunnels.

Unfortunately, in October 2001, The Government placed *Railtrack* into administration and it remains to be seen what, if any, of the above renewal programmes will see the light of day.

Feasibility work is being carried out for Phase 2 projects and, perhaps, exciting times still possibly lie ahead. We will, therefore, have to wait and see if the above proposals come to fruition and whether a revision of this volume of Line By Line will be needed!

Now, please turn the page and trace the East Coast Main Line northwards from London King's Cross station - Line By Line.

# LEGEND

## An Overview

In compiling this book, the route has been split into five-mile sections, with one section per page. Each section comprises:

- A gradient profile
- A track plan
- A photograph

## The Gradient Profiles

These show a 'cutaway' side-on view of the section, exaggerated enough to clearly show the changing gradients of the route. There is also a vertical scale, marked in 200 foot increments; the highest point on the route is Cobbinshaw Summit which is 880ft. above sea level while the two highest points on the ECML itself are 400ft. and 345ft. at Grantshouse and Stoke, respectively.

## The Track Plans

These show a 'birds eye' view of the route, with running lines, junctions, etc. clearly marked. It should be noted that these plans are schematic and, while the maps themselves are to scale, certain features have had to be slightly enlarged to maintain clarity.

## Key to Symbols

To make the diagrams in the following pages easy to use, symbols and abbreviations have been kept to the absolute minimum:

| | | | | |
|---|---|---|---|---|
| ▬▬▬ | = station platform (in use) | *U.G.L.* | = | Up Goods Loop |
| ▭ | = station platform (disused) | *D.G.L.* | = | Down Goods Loop |
| SB | = signal box | *U.P.L.* | = | Up Passenger Loop |
| PSB | = power signal box | *D.P.L.* | = | Down Passenger Loop |
| ⊠ | = disused signal box | ⋮ | = | boundary between signal box areas |

King's Cross
to
Berwick-upon-Tweed

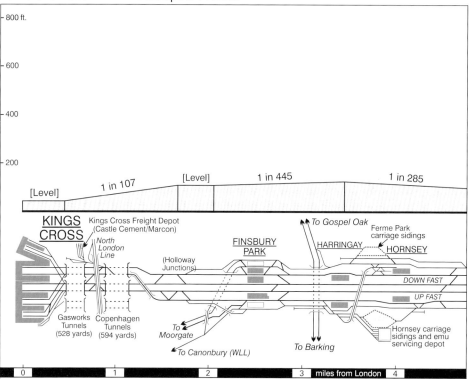

- 800 ft.
- 600
- 400
- 200

[Level]    1 in 107    [Level]    1 in 445    1 in 285

**KINGS CROSS**

Kings Cross Freight Depot
(Castle Cement/Marcon)

North London Line

(Holloway Junctions)

To Gospel Oak
Ferme Park carriage sidings

**FINSBURY PARK**

HARRINGAY

HORNSEY

DOWN FAST

UP FAST

Gasworks Tunnels (528 yards)

Copenhagen Tunnels (594 yards)

To Moorgate

To Canonbury (WLL)

To Barking

Hornsey carriage sidings and emu servicing depot

0    1    2    3   miles from London   4

**LONDON KING'S CROSS** : This is the start of our journey down the East Coast Main Line, King's Cross station, where two class 91 locomotives also wait to leave the terminus on their own journey with GNER services to the north; 91004 *Grantham* and 91026 *York Minster*, respectively. (MB 08/00)

12

**GASWORKS TUNNELS** : The rear power car (43038) of the HST forming 1S30, the 1400 King's Cross to Aberdeen disappears into the centre bore of Gasworks Tunnels; the west bore is still used by local EMU services, but the east bore is no longer in use. (MB 08/00)

**HORNSEY** : A brief reminder of a golden era when the classic 'Deltic' locomotives used to ply their trade on inter-city expresses up and down the ECML between London and Edinburgh. Privately owned 55019 *Royal Highland Fusilier* passes through Hornsey in charge of charter 1Z46, the 1503 King's cross to York, unfortunately displaying an incorrect headcode! Ferme Park is visible on the right of the picture. (NG 05/99)

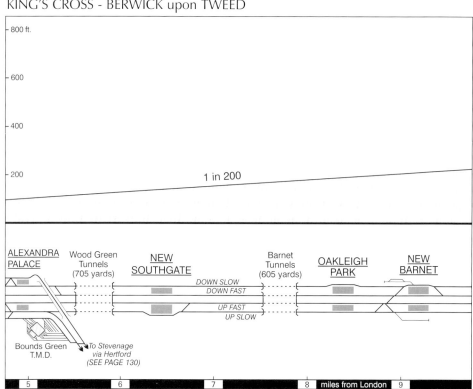

- 800 ft.

- 600

- 400

- 200

1 in 200

ALEXANDRA PALACE

Wood Green Tunnels (705 yards)

NEW SOUTHGATE

DOWN SLOW

DOWN FAST

UP FAST

UP SLOW

Barnet Tunnels (605 yards)

OAKLEIGH PARK

NEW BARNET

Bounds Green T.M.D.

To Stevenage via Hertford (SEE PAGE 130)

5    6    7    8   miles from London   9

**ALEXANDRA PALACE** : Contrasting unit designs! As 313041 pauses at Alexandra Palace to pick up a solitary passenger while working the 1242 Moorgate to Welwyn Garden City, 365522 passes on the centre road with the 1251 King's Cross to Cambridge. (BM 09/00)

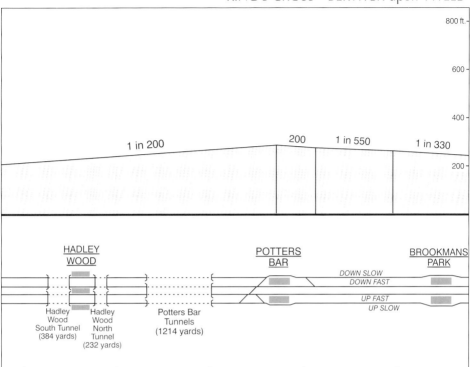

800 ft.

600

400

1 in 200          200     1 in 550          1 in 330

200

HADLEY
WOOD

POTTERS
BAR

BROOKMANS
PARK

DOWN SLOW
DOWN FAST

UP FAST
UP SLOW

Hadley
Wood
South Tunnel
(384 yards)

Hadley
Wood
North
Tunnel
(232 yards)

Potters Bar
Tunnels
(1214 yards)

10      11      12      13  miles from London  14

**HADLEY WOOD** : Two outer-suburban services bound for King's Cross have emerged from Hadley Wood North 'up' Tunnel and into Hadley Wood station in the shape of two class 317 units, 317334 and 317372, working from Peterborough and King's Lynn, respectively. (BM 02/98)

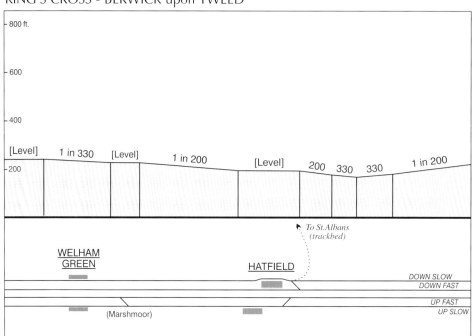

**HATFIELD** : In unpainted 'ghost' livery, 313033 calls at the staggered 'up' platform of Hatfield station, while working the 0748 Welwyn Garden City to Moorgate service. (MR 03/00)

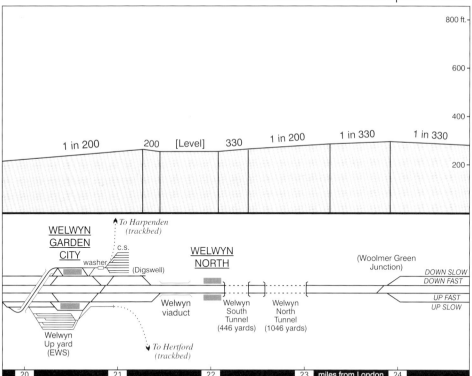

**WELWYN NORTH** : Welwyn North station is situated right in the middle of the two track section, stopping services contributing to the rush-hour congestion. Outside 'peak' periods, a handful of freight services can be seen including 6E86, the Ripple Lane to Immingham empty newsprint vans, seen here passing through the station with 56115 in charge. (MR 03/00)

**WELWYN GARDEN CITY** : These photographs offer contrasting views of Welwyn Garden City station. An elevated view shows 90019 *Penny Black* (above) speeding along the 'down' fast line with 1D35, the 0910 King's Cross to Leeds, a working regularly in the hands of a class 90 locomotive. (MR 03/00)

Back at ground level, a more conventional view sees an HST (below) proceeding 'down' the main line at the station with 1S24, the 1200 King's Cross to Inverness "*Highland Chieftain.*" (BB 09/01)

**WELWYN VIADUCT** : The main reason for the two track section between Digswell and Woolmer Green is the impressive Welwyn viaduct, seen here in two contrasting photographs. On top of the viaduct itself, 91006 (above) heads a GNER service from King's Cross to Newcastle. (BM 10/96)

A more panoramic view sees a single 317 unit (below) crossing the viaduct, the most prominent public work in Hertfordshire, with the 0915 Peterborough to King's Cross service. (MR 03/00)

# KING'S CROSS - BERWICK upon TWEED

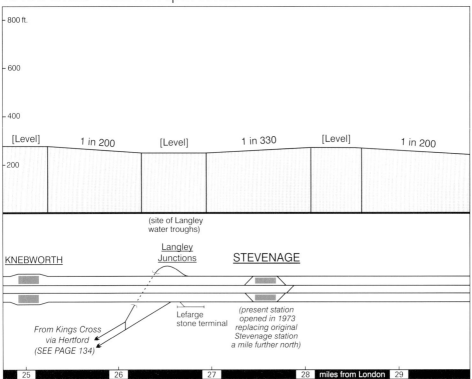

- 800 ft.
- 600
- 400
- 200

[Level] | 1 in 200 | [Level] | 1 in 330 | [Level] | 1 in 200

(site of Langley water troughs)

KNEBWORTH

Langley Junctions

STEVENAGE

Lefarge stone terminal

*(present station opened in 1973 replacing original Stevenage station a mile further north)*

*From Kings Cross via Hertford (SEE PAGE 134)*

25 | 26 | 27 | 28 | miles from London | 29

**KNEBWORTH** : As there is only a connection to the stone terminal at Langley Junction from the 'up' slow line, stone trains must first run to Welwyn Garden City to run-round. This view shows Mainline liveried 60078 passing Knebworth station with the 'empties' returning from the terminal on this weekly working. (MR 03/00)

**STEVENAGE** : The seasonal 1030 water cannon from Hornsey to Foxton and back approaches Stevenage with EWS liveried 37051 *Merehead* (above) leading and Mainline liveried 37372 on the rear. The picture clearly shows the track layout on the southern approach to the station. (BM 11/96)

'Blunt end running' of class 91 locomotives is rare and is usually restricted to the Leeds services, One such example is illustrated in this view of an unidentified class 91 (below) heading 1D39, the 1310 King's Cross to Leeds through Stevenage station. (MR 03/00)

# KING'S CROSS - BERWICK upon TWEED

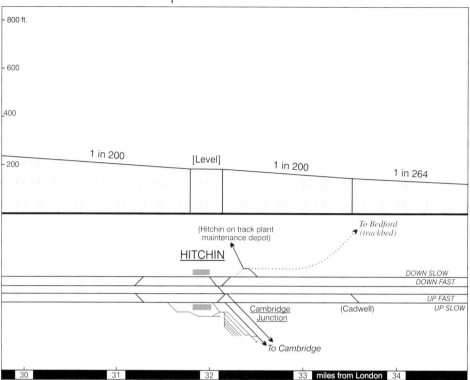

- 800 ft.
- 600
- 400
- 200

1 in 200

[Level]

1 in 200

1 in 264

(Hitchin on track plant maintenance depot)

To Bedford *(trackbed)*

### HITCHIN

DOWN SLOW
DOWN FAST
UP FAST
UP SLOW

Cambridge Junction

(Cadwell)

To Cambridge

30    31    32    33   **miles from London**   34

**HITCHIN** : The route to Royston and Cambridge leaves the ECML at Hitchin. In this view, 37712+37216 trundle through the 'up'' platform line at Hitchin station with the water cannon en-route from Royston to King's Cross Freight Terminal via HertfordNorth. (BB 10/01)

22

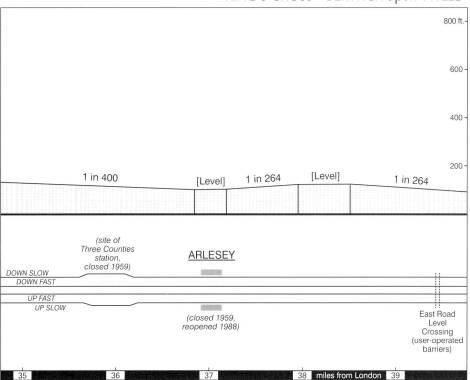

800 ft.
600
400
200

1 in 400    [Level]    1 in 264    [Level]    1 in 264

*(site of
Three Counties
station,
closed 1959)*

ARLESEY

DOWN SLOW
DOWN FAST

UP FAST
UP SLOW

*(closed 1959,
reopened 1988)*

East Road
Level
Crossing
(user-operated
barriers)

35    36    37    38    miles from London    39

**ARLESEY** : Arlesey station is served by the hourly Peterborough to London 'stoppers'. The 1315 from Peterborough is seen here arriving at the deserted station. (MR 03/00)

23

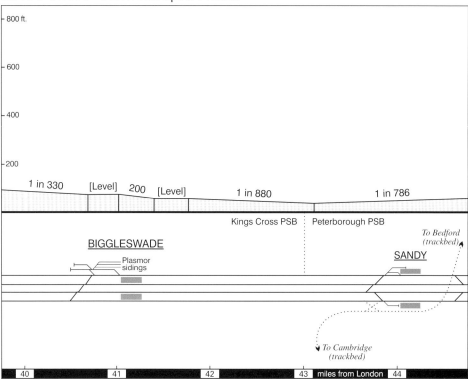

800 ft.

600

400

200

1 in 330    [Level]    *200*    [Level]    1 in 880      1 in 786

Kings Cross PSB    Peterborough PSB

*To Bedford
(trackbed)*

BIGGLESWADE

SANDY

Plasmor
sidings

*To Cambridge
(trackbed)*

40     41     42     43   miles from London   44

**BIGGLESWADE** : An unidentified class 91 speeds through Biggleswade station on 1N04, the 1430 King's Cross to Newcastle service, passing 66170 which is preparing to propel empty wagons from Bow onto a rake of empties in the Plasmor sidings. (MR 03/00)

24

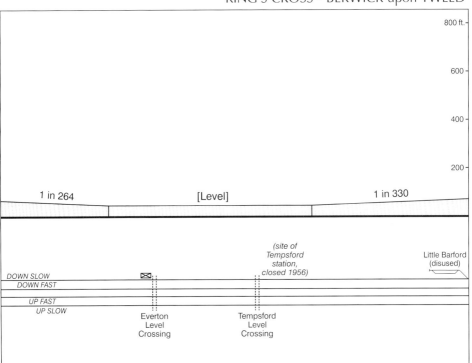

800 ft.

600

400

200

1 in 264          [Level]          1 in 330

(site of
Tempsford
station,
closed 1956)

Little Barford
(disused)

DOWN SLOW
DOWN FAST

UP FAST
UP SLOW

Everton
Level
Crossing

Tempsford
Level
Crossing

45          46          47          48  miles from London  49

**SANDY** : The station at Sandy is situated on a long sweeping curve. The 'up' platform is now situated on the site of the former Sandy & Potton Railway, which was later incorporated into a through route between Oxford and Cambridge. 66136+37379 pass through the station in charge of 6Z39, the 1450 Peterborough to Temple Mills additional engineers working. (NG 05/01)

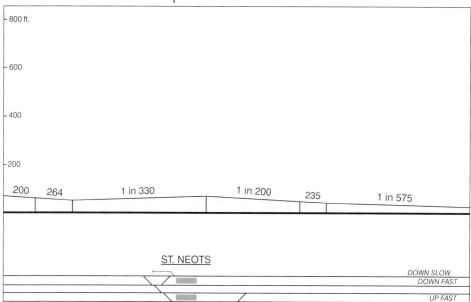

ST. NEOTS

DOWN SLOW
DOWN FAST
UP FAST
UP SLOW

| 50 | 51 | 52 | 53 | miles from London | 54 |

**ST. NEOTS** : A class 91 hauls 1S01, the 1530 King's Cross to Edinburgh, through St. Neots; the lines on the extreme left and right of the picture are the 'up' and 'down' refuge sidings, respectively. (BB 05/01)

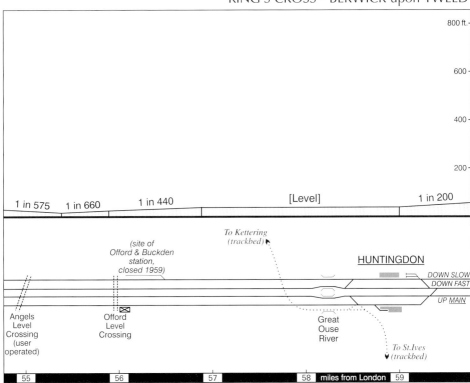

800 ft.

600

400

200

1 in 575    1 in 660    1 in 440    [Level]    1 in 200

*To Kettering*
*(trackbed)*

*(site of*
*Offord & Buckden*
*station,*
*closed 1959)*

HUNTINGDON

DOWN SLOW
DOWN FAST
UP *MAIN*

Angels
Level
Crossing
(user
operated)

Offord
Level
Crossing

Great
Ouse
River

*To St.Ives*
*(trackbed)*

55    56    57    58    miles from London    59

**HUNTINGDON** : An unidentified Vriving Van trailer (DVT) heads 1E09, the 1000 Glasgow Central to King's Cross, through Huntingdon station, where the view is spoilt by the elevated concrete bridge which carries the A14 trunk road across the main line. (BB 05/01)

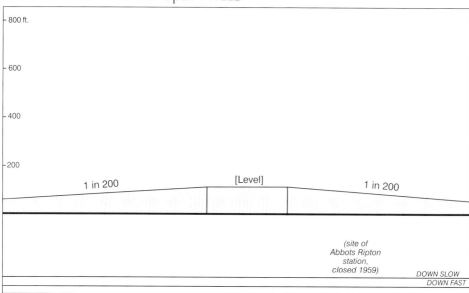

- 800 ft.

- 600

- 400

- 200

1 in 200       [Level]       1 in 200

(site of
Abbots Ripton
station,
closed 1959)

DOWN SLOW

DOWN FAST

UP MAIN

60      61      62      63   miles from London   64

**ABBOTS RIPTON** : Loadhaul liveried 56112  heads 4E25, the Bow to Heck empty Plasmor wagons through the long shallow cutting at Abbots Ripton. (BB 10/01)

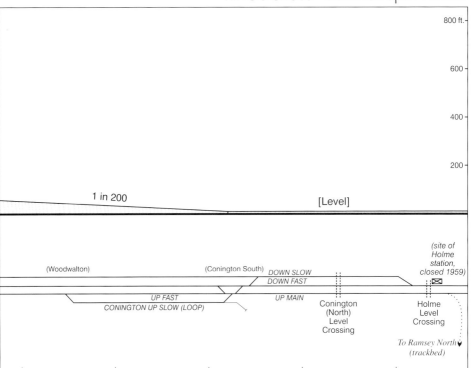

800 ft.

600

400

200

1 in 200

[Level]

(site of
Holme
station,
closed 1959)

(Woodwalton)

(Conington South) DOWN SLOW
DOWN FAST

UP FAST
CONINGTON UP SLOW (LOOP)

UP MAIN

Conington
(North)
Level
Crossing

Holme
Level
Crossing

To Ramsey North
(trackbed)

65    66    67    68  miles from London  69

**HOLME** : At Holme, the running lines converge from three to two tracks some 14 chains south of Holme gate box and level crossing, where an HST is seen passing in charge of 1E10, the 0755 Inverness to King's Cross *"Highland Chieftain"* service. (BB 09/01)

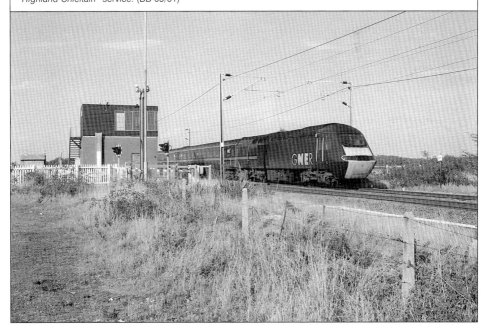

29

# KING'S CROSS - BERWICK upon TWEED

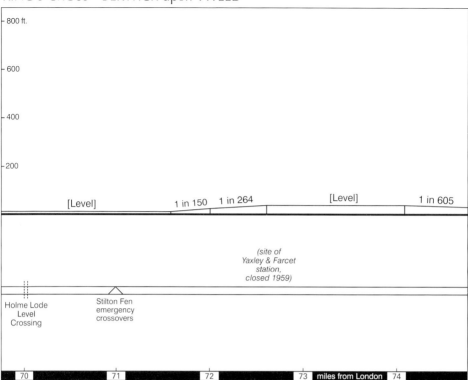

[Level]    1 in 150    1 in 264    [Level]    1 in 605

(site of
Yaxley & Farcet
station,
closed 1959)

Holme Lode
Level
Crossing

Stilton Fen
emergency
crossovers

70      71      72      73  miles from London  74

**HOLME LODE** : An impressive photograph of a pair of class 37 locomotives, with 37116 *Sister Dora* leading, making their way south at Holme with 6L79, the Doncaster Railport to Harwich 'Enterprise' service, which was uncharacteristically well loaded on this particular occasion. (JR 10/98)

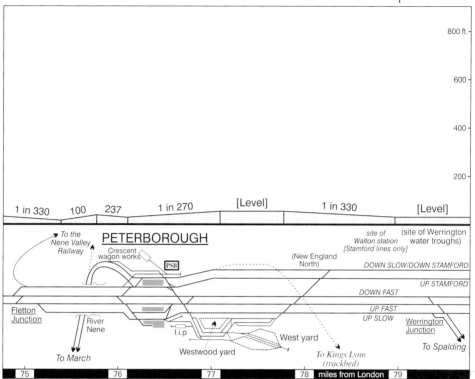

800 ft.
600
400
200

1 in 330    100    237    1 in 270    [Level]    1 in 330    [Level]

PETERBOROUGH

To the Nene Valley Railway

Crescent wagon works

PSB

Fletton Junction

River Nene

l.i.p

To March

Westwood yard

West yard

(New England North)

site of Walton station [Stamford lines only]

(site of Werrington water troughs)

DOWN SLOW/DOWN STAMFORD

UP STAMFORD

DOWN FAST

UP FAST
UP SLOW

Werrington Junction

To Spalding

To Kings Lynn (trackbed)

75    76    77    78    miles from London    79

**PETERBOROUGH** : At Crescent Junction, the line to March diverges from the ECML and passes under the main line again at Fletton Road Junction, where 158863 is seen heading east towards March on a cross-country service from Liverpool Lime Street to Norwich. (BB 05/01)

**PETERBOROUGH** : 'Presflos' were once a common sight on the ECML conveying spent fuel ash from East Midlands power stations to fill worked-out clay pits at Fletton, south of Peterborough and 58040 *Cottam Power Station* (above) is seen entering Peterborough station with a rake of empty 'Presflos'. (BM 08/94)

A freight flow which still runs is the daily cement train from Ketton to King's Cross Goods Yard. The 'empties' (6M93) pass through Peterborough hauled by another class 58 locomotive, 58032 *Thoresby Colliery* (below), where the station along with some stabled locomotives can be seen in the background. (JR 05/98)

**EASTFIELD** : When the Peterborough area was resignalled, Eastfield signalbox was retained to control access to the up sidings, which top 'n' tailed 20902 *Lorna* and 20903 *Alison* pass with a weed killing train; 56054 is also visible approaching Peterborough with 6L69, the Doncaster Yard to Biggleswade/Bow. (JR 05/97)

**WERRINGTON JUNCTION**: The main line to Spalding leaves the ECML three miles north of Peterboriugh at Werrington Junction and 90027 *Allerton T&RS Depot Quality Approved* is seen approaching the junction in charge of 1D41, the 1510 King's Cross to Leeds.(JR 03/99)

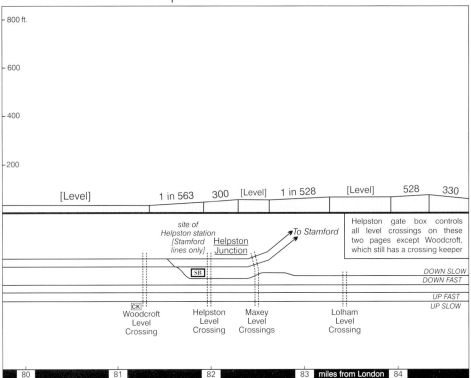

- 800 ft.
- 600
- 400
- 200

[Level]     1 in 563     300     [Level]     1 in 528     [Level]     528     330

site of
Helpston station
[Stamford     Helpston
lines only]     Junction

To Stamford

Helpston gate box controls all level crossings on these two pages except Woodcroft, which still has a crossing keeper

SB

DOWN SLOW
DOWN FAST

UP FAST
UP SLOW

CK
Woodcroft
Level
Crossing

Helpston
Level
Crossing

Maxey
Level
Crossings

Lolham
Level
Crossing

80     81     82     83  miles from London  84

**HELPSTON JUNCTION** : An unidentified train of empty 4-wheel stone hoppers approaches Helpston level crossing from the south behind 56078. The 'grid' is on the electrified 'down' slow/Stamford line, while the running lines of the ECML can be seen to the left of view. (BM 08/95)

34

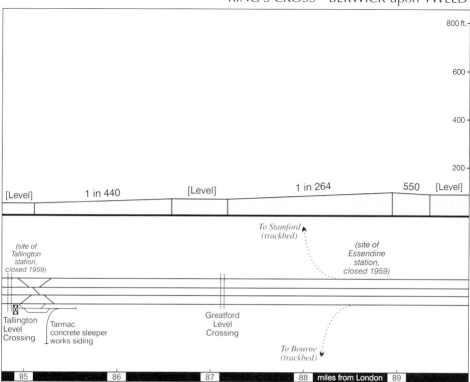

800 ft.
600
400
200

[Level]  1 in 440  [Level]  1 in 264  550  [Level]

*To Stamford*
*(trackbed)*

*(site of Tallington station, closed 1959)*

*(site of Essendine station, closed 1959)*

⊠
Tallington Level Crossing

Tarmac concrete sleeper works siding

Greatford Level Crossing

*To Bourne*
*(trackbed)*

85  86  87  88  **miles from London**  89

**TALLINGTON** : Only a meagre payload for 47016, sporting the former Railfreight grey livery and large logo, as it passes Tallington with 6L79, the Doncaster to Harwich 'Enterprise'. On the right are the sidings to Tarmac concrete works and Redland stone terminal. (JR 02/98)

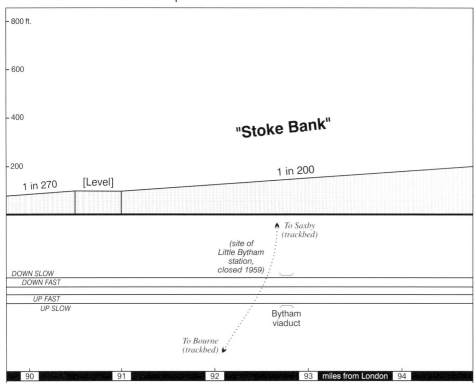

"Stoke Bank"

800 ft.

600

400

200

1 in 200

1 in 270    [Level]

To Saxby
(trackbed)

(site of
Little Bytham
station,
closed 1959)

DOWN SLOW
DOWN FAST

UP FAST
UP SLOW

Bytham
viaduct

To Bourne
(trackbed)

90    91    92    93    miles from London    94

**LITTLE BYTHAM** : The quaint village of Little Bytham has a public house by the side of the ECML aptly named 'The Mallard' after the famous Gresley pacific steam locomotive. It was on 3rd July 1938 when *Mallard* clocked up a speed of 126mph, generally acknowledged as the world record for steam. This photograph shows an unidentified class 91 crossing the viaduct with 1D43, the 1610 King's Cross to Leeds, (BB 09/01)

36

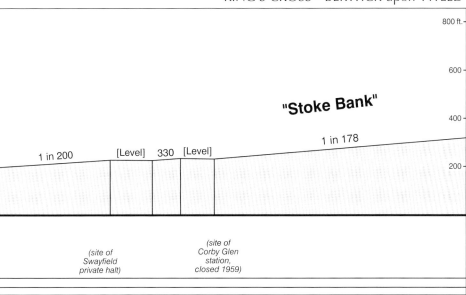

800 ft.

600

"Stoke Bank"

400

1 in 178

1 in 200          [Level]    330   [Level]

200

(site of
Swayfield
private halt)

(site of
Corby Glen
station,
closed 1959)

95          96          97          98   miles from London   99

BURTON Le COGGLES : A Central Trains class 158 unit (158847) crosses a bridge at Burton Le Coggles near Corby Glen with a service from Norwich to Liverpool Lime Street. (CB 04/00)

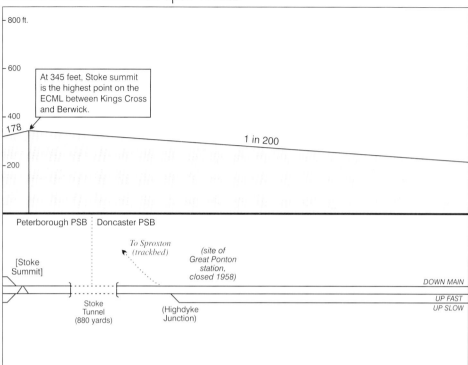

- 800 ft.
- 600
- 400
- 178
- 200

At 345 feet, Stoke summit is the highest point on the ECML between Kings Cross and Berwick.

1 in 200

Peterborough PSB ┊ Doncaster PSB

To Sproxton
(trackbed)

(site of
Great Ponton
station,
closed 1958)

[Stoke
Summit]

DOWN MAIN

Stoke
Tunnel
(880 yards)

(Highdyke
Junction)

UP FAST
UP SLOW

100     101     102     103  miles from London  104

**STOKE** : Due to engineering work on the Melton Mowbray line, services between Syston and Peterborough were diverted via the ECML in April 2000. One such service, a stone working from Mountsorrel to Peterborough, was recorded in the cutting on the approach to Stoke Tunnel behind 60004. (CB 04/00)

38

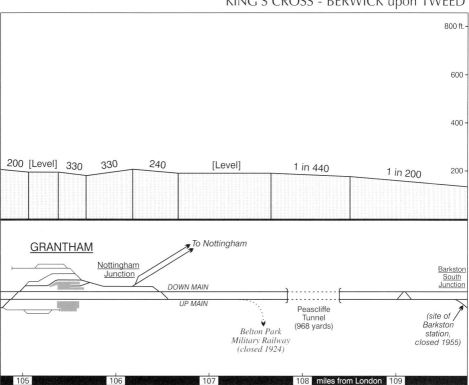

800 ft.

600

400

200 [Level]   330   330   240   [Level]   1 in 440   1 in 200   200

GRANTHAM

To Nottingham

Nottingham
Junction

DOWN MAIN

UP MAIN

Barkston
South
Junction

Belton Park
Military Railway
(closed 1924)

Peascliffe
Tunnel
(968 yards)

(site of
Barkston
station,
closed 1955)

105   106   107   108   miles from London   109

**GRANTHAM** : The up and down fast lines at Grantham are also the main platform roads and 66120 can be seen heading through the station with a lightweight 4L73, the Doncaster Railport to Harwich 'Intermodal'. (MB 07/00)

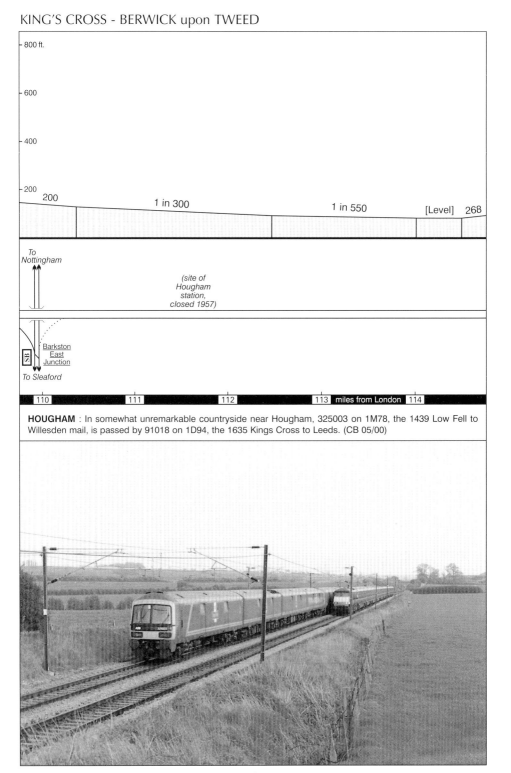

- 800 ft.

- 600

- 400

- 200
200

1 in 300

1 in 550

[Level]

268

To Nottingham

(site of Hougham station, closed 1957)

Barkston East Junction

SB

To Sleaford

110    111    112    113  miles from London  114

**HOUGHAM** : In somewhat unremarkable countryside near Hougham, 325003 on 1M78, the 1439 Low Fell to Willesden mail, is passed by 91018 on 1D94, the 1635 Kings Cross to Leeds. (CB 05/00)

40

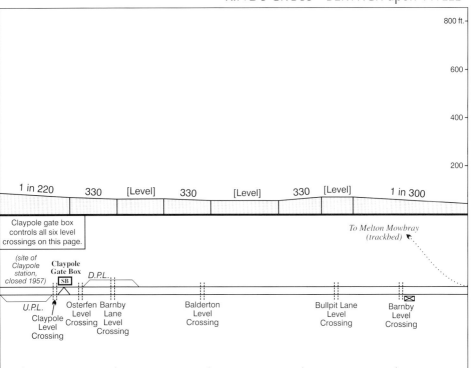

800 ft.
600
400
200

1 in 220 | 330 | [Level] | 330 | [Level] | 330 | [Level] | 1 in 300

Claypole gate box controls all six level crossings on this page.

*To Melton Mowbray (trackbed)*

*(site of Claypole station, closed 1957)*

**Claypole Gate Box**
SB

*D.P.L.*

*U.P.L.*

Claypole Level Crossing

Osterfen Level Crossing

Barnby Lane Level Crossing

Balderton Level Crossing

Bullpit Lane Level Crossing

Barnby Level Crossing

115 | 116 | 117 | 118 miles from London | 119

**CLAYPOLE** : EWS-liveried 37694 approaches Barnby Lane crossing, Claypole, on 7H21, the 1614 Doncaster to Peterborough departmental service conveying, on this occasion, Plasser units and continuous welded rails bound for Peterborough. The line in the foreground is the 'down' passenger loop. (CB 04/00)

**NEWARK FLAT CROSSING** : The famous crossing at Newark is the centrepiece of these two photographs. 56113 (above) is about to join the ECML at Newark Crossing South Junction having come off the Lincoln line with a rake of cargowagons conveying newsprint; 6L71, the Immingham Dock to Ripple Lane. (CB 03/00)

A 100mph speed restriction is clearly in place at the crossing itself, where 82229 (below) is seen heading south with 1A17, the 1105 Leeds to King's Cross. This photograph shows the construction, on site, of the new bridge to replace the existing structure across the River Trent. (CB 03/00)

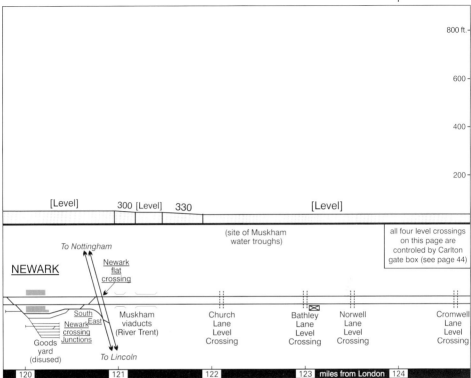

800 ft.

600

400

200

[Level]    300 [Level]    330    [Level]

(site of Muskham water troughs)

all four level crossings on this page are controled by Carlton gate box (see page 44)

*To Nottingham*

Newark flat crossing

## NEWARK

South Newark crossing East Junctions

Goods yard (disused)

*To Lincoln*

Muskham viaducts (River Trent)

Church Lane Level Crossing

Bathley Lane Level Crossing

Norwell Lane Level Crossing

Cromwell Lane Level Crossing

| 120 | 121 | 122 | 123 | miles from London | 124 |

**NEWARK** : Newark actually boasts two stations; Newark Castle is situated on the Nottingham to Lincoln line and Newark North Gate is on the ECML. North Gate station is illustrated here, where 82220 is seen at the rear of 1S15, the 0830 King's Cross to Edinburgh. Note the well kept pot plants! (CB 03/00)

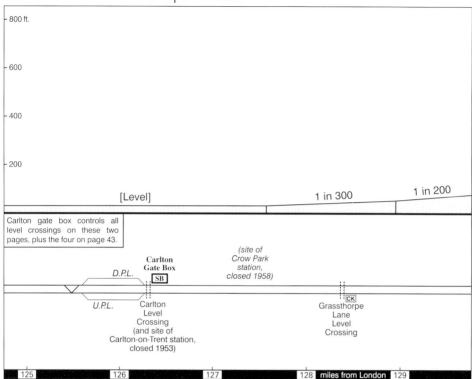

800 ft.

600

400

200

[Level]   1 in 300   1 in 200

Carlton gate box controls all level crossings on these two pages, plus the four on page 43.

D.P.L.

Carlton Gate Box

SB

*(site of Crow Park station, closed 1958)*

U.P.L.

Carlton Level Crossing (and site of Carlton-on-Trent station, closed 1953)

CK

Grassthorpe Lane Level Crossing

125   126   127   128 miles from London 129

**CARLTON** : EWS hire-in class 90 locomotives from EWS/Freightliner to cover for class 91s being overhauled at Doncaster and are used on GNER services to Leeds. One such service, 1D35, the 0910 King's Cross to Leeds, is seen passing Carlton gate box headed by 90037. The 'up' loop can be seen to the left of the train. (CB 03/00)

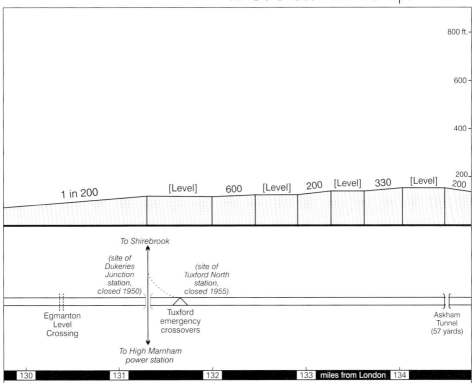

1 in 200 [Level] 600 [Level] 200 [Level] 330 [Level] 200

800 ft.
600
400
200

To Shirebrook

(site of
Dukeries
Junction
station,
closed 1950)

(site of
Tuxford North
station,
closed 1955)

Egmanton
Level
Crossing

Tuxford
emergency
crossovers

Askham
Tunnel
(57 yards)

To High Marnham
power station

130    131    132    133  miles from London  134

**ASKHAM** : This photograph could be mistaken as a section of model railway, but this is the real thing; 37717 emerges from the south portal of Askham Tunnel with 6L76, the Doncaster to Ely 'Enterprise'; a service which ran every weekday until the train was withdrawn in Autumn 2001. (CB 05/00)

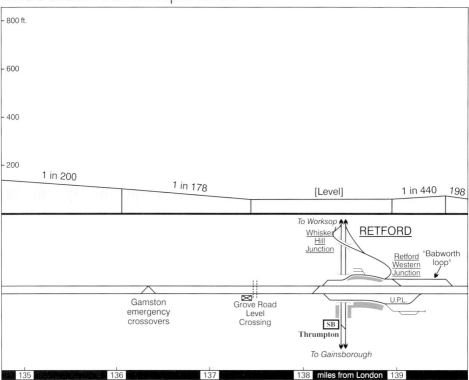

- 800 ft.
- 600
- 400
- 200

1 in 200

1 in 178

[Level]

1 in 440

198

To Worksop
Whisker
Hill
Junction

**RETFORD**

Retford
Western
Junction

"Babworth
loop"

Gamston
emergency
crossovers

Grove Road
Level
Crossing

U.P.L.

SB
Thrumpton

To Gainsborough

| 135 | 136 | 137 | 138 | miles from London | 139 |

**RETFORD WESTERN JUNCTION** : Leaving the ECML behind, 58048 negotiates Retford Western Junction and hauls 6E84, the Middleton Towers to Monk Bretton, on to the ex-Great Central line, conveying industrial sand for use in glass making. Retford station is visible above the wagons at the far right of the picture. (CB 05/96)

**RETFORD HIGH LEVEL** : The station buildings are situated alongside the up platform, while one side of an island platform (partially visible in this photograph) serves northbound passenger trains. On the up fast line, 47205 heads south with 4L85, the Leeds to Ipswich Yard freightliner. (MB 07/00)

**RETFORD LOW LEVEL** : The ex-Great Central main line between Sheffield and Gainsborough passes underneath the ECML at Retford Low Level. In this view, 66526 *Driver Steve Dunn (George)* passes the Low Level station with a Freightliner 'Heavy Haul' service (6G16) conveying imported coal from Immingham to Cottam power station. Most coal trains travel via Worksop Yard, which acts as a staging point for services to both Cottam and West Burton power stations. (CB 11/01)

- 800 ft.

- 600

- 400

- 200

1 in 198          [Level]          1 in 440

Ranskill gate box controls all
level crossings on this page,
plus Grove Road (Retford).

Ranskill
Level Crossing
(and site
of station,
closed 1958)

*(site of
Barnby Moor & Sutton
station,
closed 1949)*

*D.P.L.*

Retford
emergency
crossover

Botany Bay
Level
Crossing

Barnby Moor
Level
Crossing

Torworth
Level
Crossing

*U.P.L.*

SB
**Ranskill
Gate Box**

140        141        142        143    miles from London    144

**SCROOBY** : Aptly displaying the destination "Flower", a Serco weedkilling train formed of class 141 cars 55518+55538 pass School Lane, Scrooby, running between Doncaster and Retford. (CB 06/99)

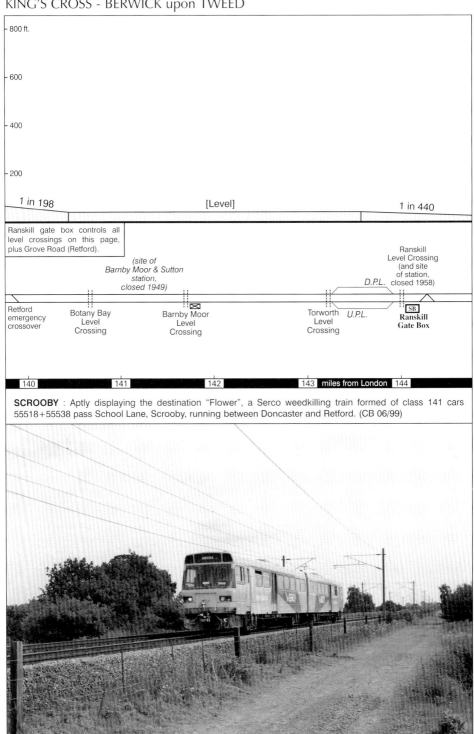

48

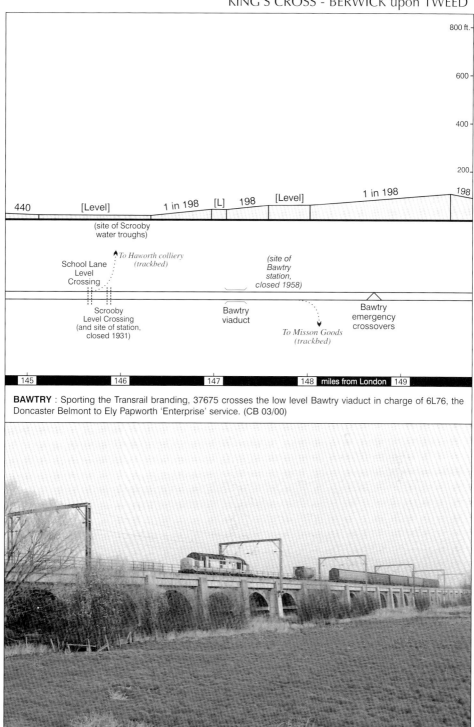

800 ft.

600

400

200

198

440     [Level]     1 in 198    [L]   198    [Level]     1 in 198

(site of Scrooby
water troughs)

*To Haworth colliery*
*(trackbed)*

School Lane
Level
Crossing

(site of
Bawtry
station,
closed 1958)

Scrooby
Level Crossing
(and site of station,
closed 1931)

Bawtry
viaduct

*To Misson Goods*
*(trackbed)*

Bawtry
emergency
crossovers

| 145 | 146 | 147 | 148 | miles from London | 149 |

**BAWTRY** : Sporting the Transrail branding, 37675 crosses the low level Bawtry viaduct in charge of 6L76, the Doncaster Belmont to Ely Papworth 'Enterprise' service. (CB 03/00)

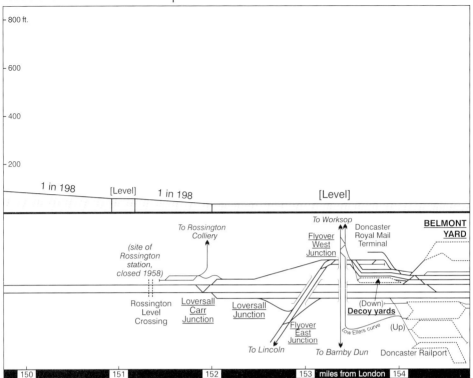

- 800 ft.
- 600
- 400
- 200

1 in 198 [Level] 1 in 198 [Level]

To Worksop

To Rossington Colliery

Flyover West Junction

Doncaster Royal Mail Terminal

**BELMONT YARD**

(site of Rossington station, closed 1958)

Rossington Level Crossing

Loversall Carr Junction

Loversall Junction

Flyover East Junction

To Lincoln

To Barnby Dun

(Down) **Decoy yards**

Low Ellers curve (Up)

Doncaster Railport

| 150 | 151 | 152 | 153 | miles from London | 154 |

**LOVERSALL CARR JUNCTION** : The returning Plasmor empties from Bow to Heck (4E25) hurry past milepost 152 at Loversall Carr Junction, in the care of 66196. The running lines to the left and right of the main line lead to Flyover East and Flyover West Junction, respectively. (CB 04/00)

50

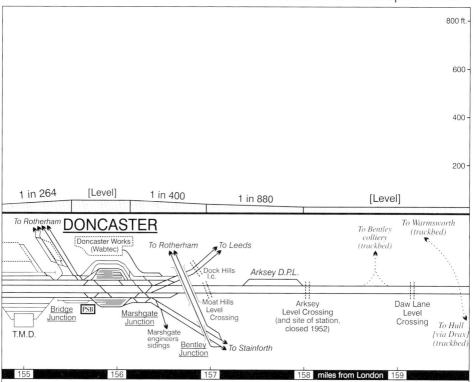

800 ft.

600

400

200

| 1 in 264 | [Level] | 1 in 400 | 1 in 880 | [Level] |

To Rotherham

**DONCASTER**

To Bentley colliery *(trackbed)*

To Warmsworth *(trackbed)*

Doncaster Works (Wabtec)

To Rotherham     To Leeds

Dock Hills l.c.

*Arksey D.P.L.*

Bridge Junction     PSB

Marshgate Junction

Moat Hills Level Crossing

Arksey Level Crossing (and site of station, closed 1952)

Daw Lane Level Crossing

To Hull [via Drax] *(trackbed)*

T.M.D.

Marshgate engineers sidings     Bentley Junction

To Stainforth

| 155 | 156 | 157 | 158 | miles from London | 159 |

**DONCASTER DECOY YARD** : A very busy scene at Doncaster Down Decoy Yard, where several locomotives can be seen: from left to right, 37698 (passing), 56089, 37801 and 66132. The single line leaving the ECML to the left of the picture gives access to the South Yorkshire Joint Line and the platform visible at the extreme right of the photograph is the Royal Mail Terminal. (CB 04/00)

**DONCASTER** : The top floor of a multi-storey car park provides an excellent bird's eye view of the layout of Doncaster station and RFS works yard. An HST (above) waits to depart from the station with 1A10, the 0700 Hull to King's Cross, "Hull Executive", whilst a GNERstar has arrived with 1X29, the 0555 King's Cross to York "White Rose" service. Behind the station is Doncaster Works, affectionately known as "The Plant." (MB 07/00)

In the works yard (below) an assortment of rolling stock can be seen along with some class 20s and 4 class 66 locomotives: 66079/66088/66085 in the foreground and 66080 in the distance. (MB 07/00)

**DONCASTER** : Doncaster is a strategic location, where main line GNER passenger services leave the ECML for the first time to serve the cities of Hull and Leeds. Waiting departure time at Doncaster is HST set 43105/112 (above) on 1A13, the 0729 Harrogate to King's Cross. (MB 07/00)

This photograph shows the vantage point for the two views opposite; namely, the multi-storey car park which is located at the north end of Doncaster station and is visible at the extreme right of this picture. Loadhaul-liveried 56077 *Thorpe Marsh Power Station* (below) is seen approaching the station with an empty MGR service returning to a South Yorkshire coal mine.(MB 08/95)

# KING'S CROSS - BERWICK upon TWEED

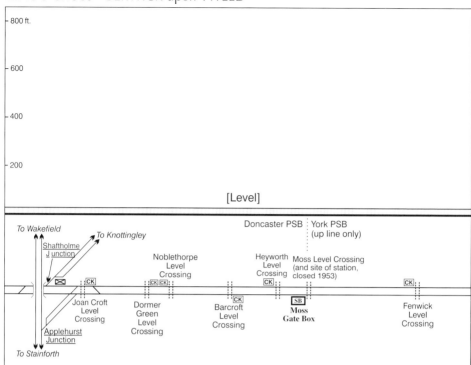

JOAN CROFT JUNCTION : Minus its *Carnedd Llewelyn* nameplate, 60034 passes Milepost 161 near Joan Croft Junction hauling 6D68, the Lindsey to Leeds loaded petroleum bogie tanks. Note the "Doncaster 5 Miles" sign in front of the electricity pylon. (CB 03/00)

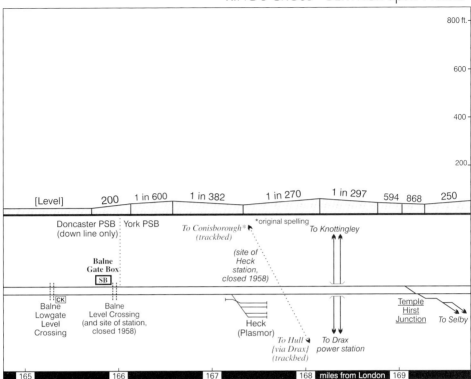

| [Level] | 200 | 1 in 600 | 1 in 382 | 1 in 270 | 1 in 297 | 594 | 868 | 250 |

Doncaster PSB
(down line only)

York PSB

*To Conisborough* *original spelling
*(trackbed)*

*To Knottingley*

**Balne Gate Box**
SB

*(site of Heck station, closed 1958)*

CK
Balne Lowgate Level Crossing

Balne Level Crossing
(and site of station, closed 1958)

Heck
(Plasmor)

*To Hull [via Drax] (trackbed)*

*To Drax* power station

Temple Hirst Junction

*To Selby*

| 165 | 166 | 167 | 168 | miles from London | 169 |

**TEMPLE HIRST JUNCTION** : The 'Selby Diversion' was constructed between Temple Hirst Junction and Colton Junction to speed up east coast services and to avoid the bottleneck of Selby, caused by its famous swing bridge. The old, non electrified, route can be seen trailing in to the right of 66123 as it negotiates Temple Hirst Junction with MGR empties from Milford to Immingham. (CB 04/00)

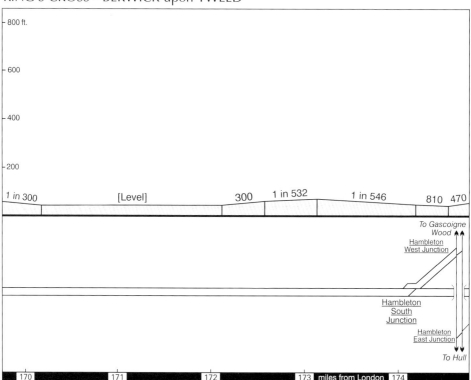

1 in 300        [Level]        300    1 in 532     1 in 546      810   470

To Gascoigne Wood

Hambleton West Junction

Hambleton South Junction

Hambleton East Junction

To Hull

170          171          172          173   miles from London   174

**HAMBLETON SOUTH JUNCTION** : The embankment visible in the background carries the main line from Leeds to Hull, from which 56038 has left to join the ECML by means of Hambleton South Curve. The train in view is 6G33, the Eggborough to Lindsey empty bogie tanks. (CB 05/00)

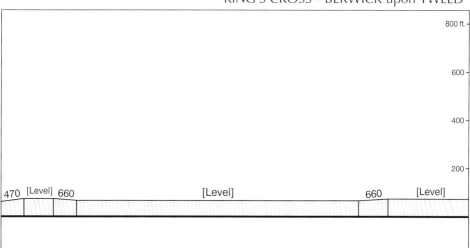

800 ft.

600

400

200

470 [Level] 660          [Level]          660    [Level]

Hambleton
North
Junction

175      176      177      178 miles from London 179

**HAMBLETON NORTH JUNCTION** : A Class 144 2-car Pacer Unit No. 144002 joins the ECML at Hambleton North Junction with a local service from Hull to York. (CB 06/00)

57

**BURN** : Res-liveried 47772 heads south along the ECML near the village of Burn with 6D65, the Selby to Doncaster Belmont 'Enterprise'. This, along with Colton Junvtion, is a very popular location amongst enthusiasts to espy and photograph an assortment of rail traffic using the ECML. (CB 11/99)

**COLTON NORTH** : Photographed from a footbridge which leads from the village of Colton to Colton Breck farm, EWS 90027 *Allerton T & RS Depot Quality Approved* approaches Colton Junction with 1M51, the 1522 Shieldmuir RMT to London mail. (MB 07/00)

**COLTON** : Colton road bridge is probably the most popular location from where enthusiasts can enjoy expansive views of passenger and freight services on the ECML plus the main line to Church Fenton; the O/S grid reference is 542432 on Landranger Map No. 105. Travelling south on the ECML, 60059 *Swinden Dalesman* (above) heads 6D11, the Tees Yard to Scunthorpe steel empties. (JR 06/99)

Looking from the opposite side of the main line, 47212 (below) passes Colton in charge of 4D87, the Wilton to Doncaster Railport freightliner. (CB 10/99)

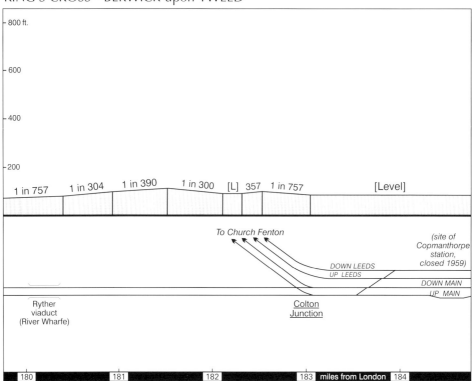

800 ft.

600

400

200

1 in 757    1 in 304    1 in 390    1 in 300   [L]   357   1 in 757      [Level]

*To Church Fenton*

*(site of Copmanthorpe station, closed 1959)*

*DOWN LEEDS*
*UP LEEDS*

*DOWN MAIN*
*UP MAIN*

Ryther viaduct (River Wharfe)

Colton Junction

180     181     182     183   **miles from London**   184

**COLTON JUNCTION** : The main line from Church Fenton joins the ECML at Colton Junction and is where we see 56081 in the process of crossing over from the 'down' Normanton to the 'down' main of the ECML itself with 6N79, the Scunthorpe to Tees Yard coke empties. (MB 07/00)

60

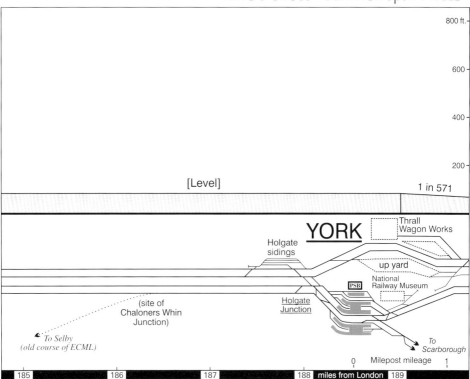

800 ft.

600

400

200

[Level]                                                          1 in 571

YORK

Holgate sidings

Thrall Wagon Works

up yard

National Railway Museum

PSB

(site of Chaloners Whin Junction)

Holgate Junction

To Selby (old course of ECML)

To Scarborough

0   Milepost mileage   1

185    186    187    188  miles from London  189

**CHALONERS WHIN** : Prior to the construction of the 'Selby Diversion', the ECML used to join the main line from Leeds at Chaloners Whin, some two miles south of York. A supermarket has now been built on the site, which can be seen behind the two passing trains. Whilst 56081 heads back to Redcar with coke empties, 66210 speeds south with 6V02, the Thrislington to Margam containerised limestone. The course of the old ECML is now a path and cycle route. (MB 07/00)

**YORK DRINGHOUSES** : A marshalling yard, complete with 'hump', was situated on the up side of the main line at Dringhouses. A development of luxury houses has been built on the site where 66112 passes with 6V49, the Lynemouth to Newport Docks conveying Aluminium ingots. (MB 07/00)

**YORK YARD NORTH** : This view shows the ECML sweepinground to York station on the left, the expansive carriage & wagon works in the background and BSC-liveried 60033 Tees Steel Express coming off the 'station avoiding' line at York North with 6N02, the Humber to Jarrow loaded bogie tanks. (CB/00)

**YORK** : The station at York is one of the noblest pieces of architecture in the land and is situated on a loop line turning fully through 150º. During electrification, the overhead catenary was constructed unobtrusively, as can be seen to good effect in this photograph (above) which also illustrates the magnificent canopy and where the through running lines were once situated. (MB 08/01)

At the north end of the station, we see an end-on view of the trainshed canopy, beneath which 91015 (below) departs with 1S28, the 1300 King's cross to Edinburgh. (CB 04/00)

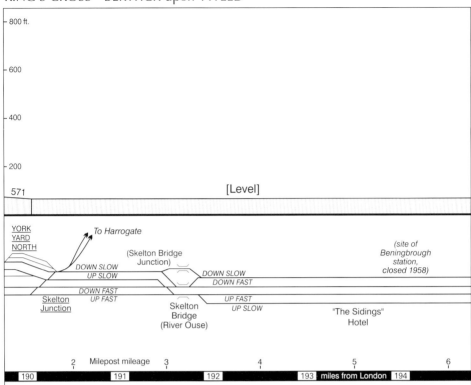

- 800 ft.
- 600
- 400
- 200

571                                         [Level]

YORK YARD NORTH

To Harrogate

(Skelton Bridge Junction)

(site of Beningbrough station, closed 1958)

DOWN SLOW
UP SLOW
DOWN SLOW
DOWN FAST

DOWN FAST
UP FAST
UP FAST
UP SLOW

Skelton Junction

Skelton Bridge (River Ouse)

"The Sidings" Hotel

2    Milepost mileage    3                      4                  5                  6

190                 191                 192           193    miles from London    194

**SHIPTON** : Mainline liveried 60011 heads 6M79, the Redcar to Clitheroe coal train along the 'up' slow line and approaches the "Edinburgh 200 Miles" sign at Shipton by Benningborough. Just visible above the double-yellow signal is 'The Sidings' hotel and restaurant; a very popular location with railway enthusiasts! (MR 04/00)

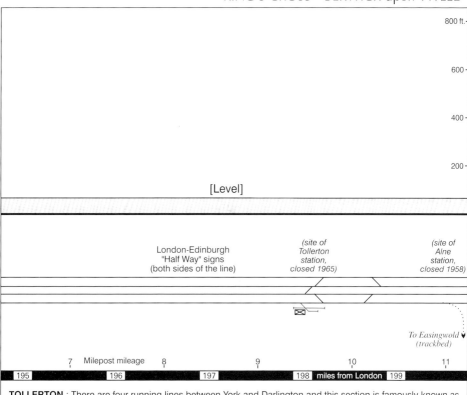

800 ft.

600

400

200

[Level]

London-Edinburgh
"Half Way" signs
(both sides of the line)

*(site of*
*Tollerton*
*station,*
*closed 1965)*

*(site of*
*Alne*
*station,*
*closed 1958)*

*To Easingwold*
*(trackbed)*

7    Milepost mileage    8                    9                    10                    11

| 195 | 196 | 197 | 198 | miles from London | 199 |

**TOLLERTON** : There are four running lines between York and Darlington and this section is famously known as the 'Racing Stretch' as it has always been associated with fast running and train performance, especially in the days of steam. This view shows 56105 on 4L79, the Wilton to Felixstowe freightliner proceeding along the up slow line, well laden with deep-sea containers. (MR 04/97)

65

# KING'S CROSS - BERWICK upon TWEED

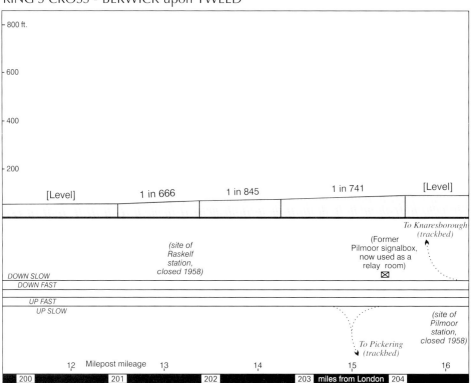

- 800 ft.
- 600
- 400
- 200

[Level]    1 in 666    1 in 845    1 in 741    [Level]

*To Knaresborough (trackbed)*

(Former Pilmoor signalbox, now used as a relay room) ⊠

*(site of Raskelf station, closed 1958)*

DOWN SLOW
DOWN FAST

UP FAST
UP SLOW

*To Pickering (trackbed)*

*(site of Pilmoor station, closed 1958)*

Milepost mileage   12   13   14   15   16

200   201   202   203   miles from London   204

**RASKELF** : The late evening sun catches 56083 as it heads north on the 'down' slow line at Raskelf with 6E09, the Etruria to Tees Yard loaded steel sections. This train ceased to run in the summer of 2000 following the closure of Shelton (Etruria) steelworks. (MR 04/97)

66

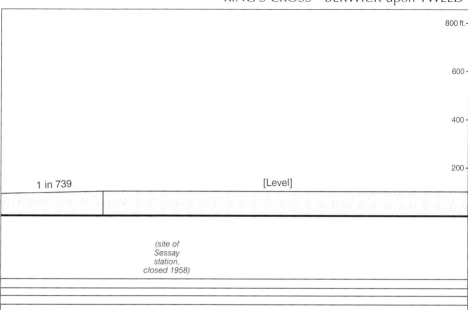

800 ft.
600
400
200

1 in 739                                         [Level]

(site of
Sessay
station,
closed 1958)

17    Milepost mileage    18              19              20              21
205              206                    207              208  miles from London  209

**SOWERBY** : A motley selection of HEA coal hoppers forming 6D78, the Redcar to Scunthorpe sinter train is seen at Sowerby on the southern outskirts of Thirsk hauled by 60010. (MR 04/00)

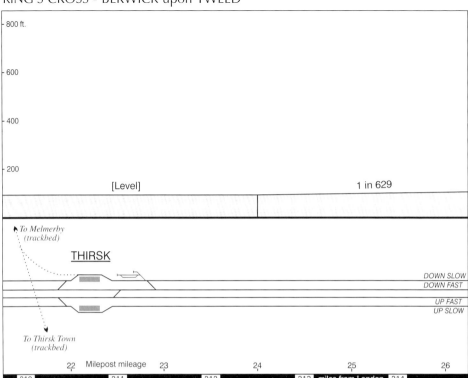

- 800 ft.
- 600
- 400
- 200

[Level]                                          1 in 629

*To Melmerby*
*(trackbed)*

## THIRSK

DOWN SLOW
DOWN FAST

UP FAST
UP SLOW

*To Thirsk Town*
*(trackbed)*

22  Milepost mileage  23          24          25          26

210          211          212          213  miles from London  214

**THIRSK** : Prior to the introduction of class 67s, 1V64, the 1406 Low fell to Plymouth mail train was booked for a pair of 47/7s for loco balancing purposes. In this view, 47767 *Saint Columba* + 47787 *Victim Support* speed through Thirsk station, where track rationalisation has resulted in the platforms being only accessible to trains on the up and down slow lines. (MR 04/00)

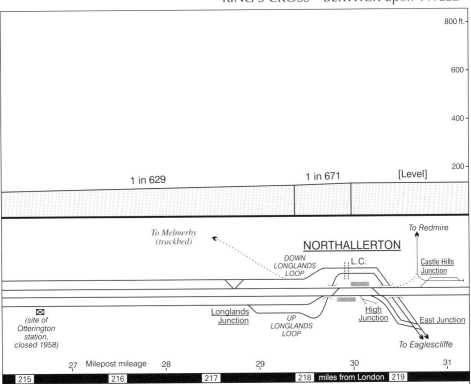

800 ft.

600

400

200

1 in 629          1 in 671          [Level]

*To Melmerby
(trackbed)*

↖

**NORTHALLERTON**

↑ *To Redmire*

DOWN
*LONGLANDS
LOOP*          L.C.

Castle Hills
Junction

✉
*(site of
Otterington
station,
closed 1958)*

Longlands
Junction

*UP
LONGLANDS
LOOP*

High
Junction

East Junction

*To Eaglescliffe*

27   Milepost mileage   28          29          30          31

215          216          217          218 | miles from London | 219

**OTTERINGTON** : Sporting  Freightliner green and yellow corporate colours, 66501approaches the preserved signalbox and station buildings at South Otterington whilst at work on 4N88, the Doncaster Railport to WIlton freightliner. The train is seen unusually on the down fast line as daytime freight is almost invariably kept on the slow lines between York and Northallerton. (MR 04/00)

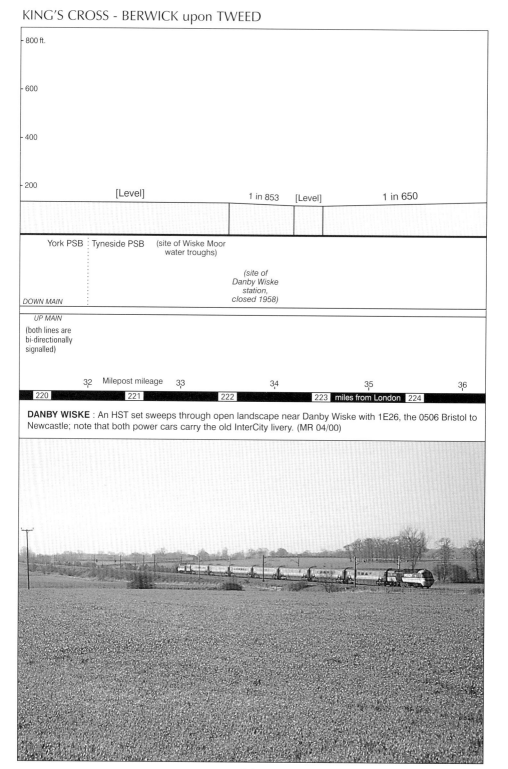

- 800 ft.
- 600
- 400
- 200

| [Level] | 1 in 853 | [Level] | 1 in 650 |

York PSB : Tyneside PSB (site of Wiske Moor water troughs)

*(site of Danby Wiske station, closed 1958)*

DOWN MAIN

UP MAIN
(both lines are bi-directionally signalled)

32   Milepost mileage   33     34     35     36

| 220 | 221 | 222 | 223 | miles from London | 224 |

**DANBY WISKE** : An HST set sweeps through open landscape near Danby Wiske with 1E26, the 0506 Bristol to Newcastle; note that both power cars carry the old InterCity livery. (MR 04/00)

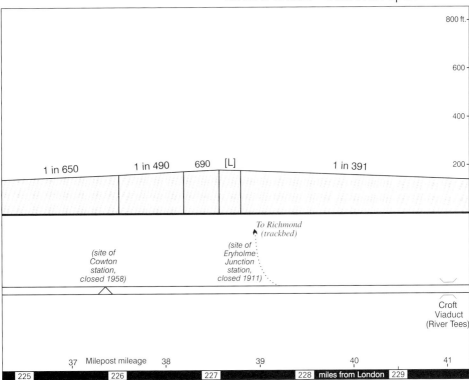

1 in 650    1 in 490    690    [L]    1 in 391

*To Richmond*
*(trackbed)*

*(site of Cowton station, closed 1958)*

*(site of Eryholme Junction station, closed 1911)*

Croft Viaduct (River Tees)

37    Milepost mileage    38    39    40    41

225    226    227    228    miles from London    229

**EAST COWTON** : Passenger services between Edinburgh and Kings Cross are booked for class 91 + Mk. 4s operation with HSTs being restricted to use on the non-electrified routes, such as Aberdeen and Harrogate, for example. This view shows the only exception to this strategy, being the booked HST working 1E03, the 0700 Edinburgh to King's Cross service near the village of East Cowton. (MR 04/00)

# KING'S CROSS - BERWICK upon TWEED

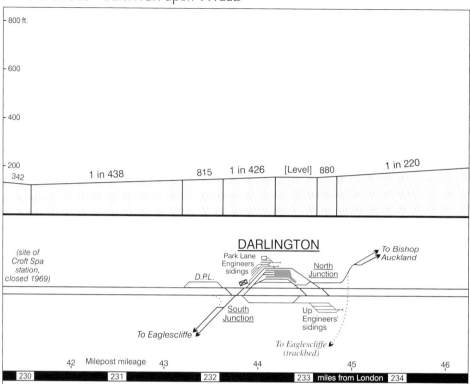

DARLINGTON : Home of the Stockton & Darlington Railway and where it all began in 1825. The station still retains its magnificent canopies spanning the platforms; the two outermost platforms are used by GNER services. The two unelectrified bay platform lines are used for local services to Tees-side and the coastal route to Sunderland, from where 142078 leaves with a service to Saltburn. (KS 09/01)

72

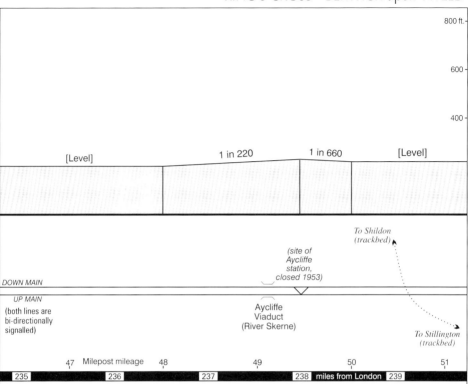

800 ft.

600

400

[Level]      1 in 220      1 in 660      [Level]

*To Shildon
(trackbed)*

*(site of
Aycliffe
station,
closed 1953)*

DOWN MAIN

UP MAIN
(both lines are
bi-directionally
signalled)

Aycliffe
Viaduct
(River Skerne)

*To Stillington
(trackbed)*

47   Milepost mileage   48     49     50     51

235    236    237    238   miles from London   239

**AYCLIFFE** : Formed of 5 mail vans, 1V64, the 1403 Low Fell to Plymouth Postal, is seen at Aycliffe, County Durham, top 'n' tailed by 47761 (leading) and 47757 at the rear. (PJR 05/99)

73

KING'S CROSS - BERWICK upon TWEED

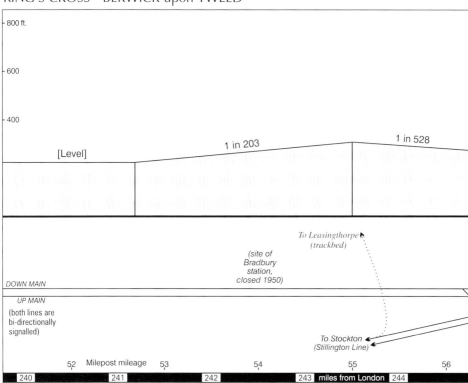

800 ft.

600

400

[Level]     1 in 203     1 in 528

*To Leasingthorpe*
*(trackbed)*

(site of
Bradbury
station,
closed 1950)

DOWN MAIN

UP MAIN
(both lines are
bi-directionally
signalled)

*To Stockton*
*(Stillington Line)*

52     Milepost mileage     53          54          55          56

240          241          242          243   miles from London   244

**FERRYHILL** : Although there is an operational signalbox at Ferryhill, it no longer controls the running lines at this point, being responsible instead for the 'Stillington Branch' to Teesside. 66068 passes the 'box' on the down fast with an empty MGR working from Drax power station to Tyne Yard. (MR 04/00)

74

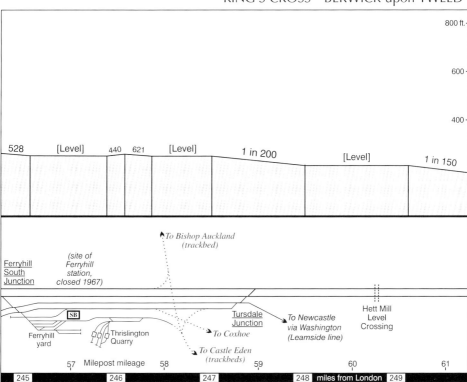

800 ft.

600

400

528    [Level]    440   621    [Level]    1 in 200    [Level]    1 in 150

To Bishop Auckland
(trackbed)

Ferryhill
South
Junction

(site of
Ferryhill
station,
closed 1967)

SB

Ferryhill
yard

Thrislington
Quarry

Tursdale
Junction

To Coxhoe

To Castle Eden
(trackbeds)

To Newcastle
via Washington
(Leamside line)

Hett Mill
Level
Crossing

57    Milepost mileage    58     59     60     61

245    246    247    248   miles from London   249

**THRISLINGTON** : The huge Steetly Quarry at Thrislington (north of Ferryhill) is situated on the 'up' side of the ECML and despatches a high proportion of Lime by rail, which includes a local trip to the Redland magnesia works at Hartlepool. This 'trip' (6P62) is seen at the loading point at Thrislington headed by 56117. (KS 05/97)

75

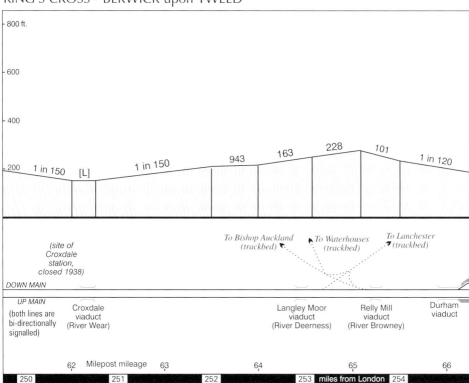

800 ft.

600

400

228
163
101
943    1 in 120
200  1 in 150  [L]    1 in 150

*To Bishop Auckland*  ➤*To Waterhouses*  *To Lanchester*
*(trackbed)* ➤  *(trackbed)*  ➤*(trackbed)*

(site of
Croxdale
station,
closed 1938)

DOWN MAIN

UP MAIN
(both lines are      Croxdale                Langley Moor        Relly Mill           Durham
bi-directionally     viaduct                 viaduct             viaduct              viaduct
signalled)           (River Wear)            (River Deerness)    (River Browney)

62    Milepost mileage    63            64                  65                   66

250           251            252            253 miles from London 254

DURHAM VIADUCT : This magnificent structure is one of four viaducts situated in this 5-mile section and is
located immediately south of Durham station. It is best viewed from the 'down' side of the main line as can be
seen in this picture of 47831 *Bolton Wanderer* on the viaduct, slowing for the Durham station stop, in charge of
1E25, the 0855 (Sun) Derby to Newcastle, , (KS 01/99)

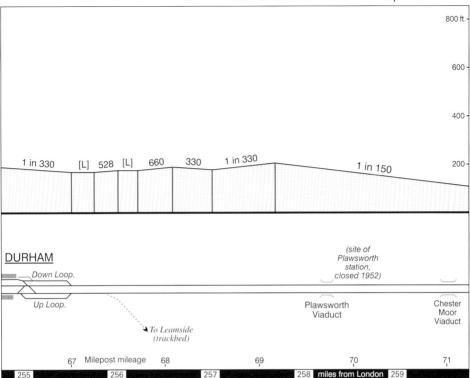

800 ft.
600
400
200

1 in 330    [L]  528  [L]   660    330    1 in 330                    1 in 150

DURHAM

Down Loop.

Up Loop.

*To Leamside*
*(trackbed)*

(site of
Plawsworth
station,
closed 1952)

Plawsworth
Viaduct

Chester
Moor
Viaduct

67   Milepost mileage   68              69              70              71

255           256              257           258  miles from London  259

**DURHAM** : The station at Durham was opened by the North Eastern Railway in 1857 and is now a Grade 2 listed building. The stylish canopy on the platform dominates this view of 66090+56062 passing through Durham station on the 'down' fast line with a departmental service working from Doncaster to Tyne Yard in readiness for some weekend engineering work in the North East. (KS 10/01)

# KING'S CROSS - BERWICK upon TWEED

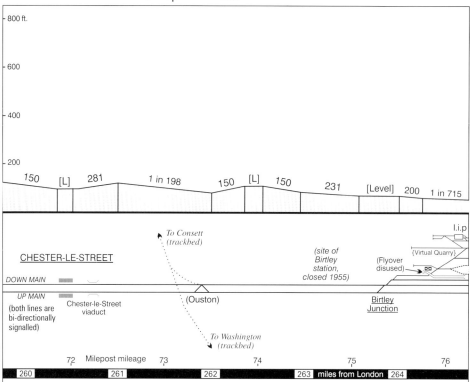

800 ft.

600

400

200

150   [L]   281    1 in 198    150   [L]   150    231    [Level]   200   1 in 715

*To Consett*
*(trackbed)*

l.i.p

CHESTER-LE-STREET

{Virtual Quarry}

(site of
Birtley
station,
closed 1955)

(Flyover
disused)

DOWN MAIN

UP MAIN

(both lines are
bi-directionally
signalled)

Chester-le-Street
viaduct

(Ouston)

Birtley
Junction

*To Washington*
*(trackbed)*

72   Milepost mileage   73      74      75      76

260      261      262      263   miles from London   264

**CHESTER-LE-STREET** : A foretaste of things to come! Prior to introduction on Virgin cross-country services, a new Voyager unit passes through Chester-Le-Street station on a special working for driver training; 5Z64 running from Newcastle to Derby and Barton Under Needwood. (KS 09/01)

78

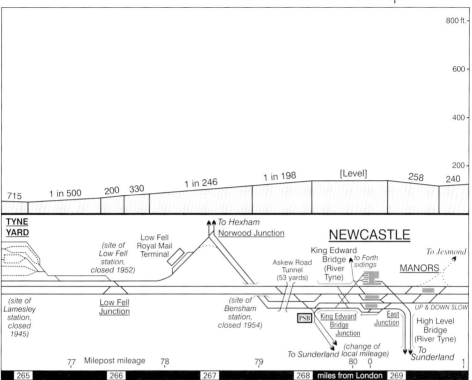

*Gradient profile (top to bottom):*

800 ft.
600
400
200

[Level]   258   240

715   1 in 500   200   330   1 in 246   1 in 198   258   240

**TYNE YARD**

To Hexham / Norwood Junction

Low Fell Royal Mail Terminal

(site of Low Fell station, closed 1952)

## NEWCASTLE

King Edward Bridge (River Tyne) → to Forth sidings

Askew Road Tunnel (53 yards)

To Jesmond

MANORS

(site of Lamesley station, closed 1945)

Low Fell Junction

(site of Bensham station, closed 1954)

PSB   King Edward Bridge Junction   East Junction

UP & DOWN SLOW

High Level Bridge (River Tyne)

To Sunderland (change of local mileage)

To Sunderland

77   Milepost mileage   78   79   80   0   1

265   266   267   268   miles from London   269

**BIRTLEY** : As an HST heads north in the distance on 1E30, the 1016 Birmingham International to Newcastle, 86417, with 67029 at the rear, passes Birtley with 1V64, the 1406 Low Fell to Plymouth mail. On the horizon, the 'Angel of the North' can just be made out. (KS 02/01)

**TYNE YARD** : Despite track rationalisation in recent years, Tyne yard is still a major freight yard used primarily to stage MGR coal trains and departmental services. Four floodlights stand proudly over the yard where 56062 prepares to leave on 6M57, the Tees Dock to Carlisle Yard Enterprise service while, in the background, a class 37 waits to trip a rake of Alumina tanks to North Blyth. (KS 04/99)

**LOW FELL** :  On an overcast day, a pair of class 67 locomotives (67017+67003) traverse the single line spur which leads from Low Fell Royal Mail terminal to join the ECML at Low fell Junction with 1V64, the 1406 Low Fell to Plymouth mail. (KS 05/00)

**NEWCASTLE UPON TYNE** : This is *the* classic view of Newcastle photographed from the castle keep, which depicts a GNER service, 1E06, the 0930 Edinburgh to King's Cross snaking its way into Newcastle Central station propelled by 91004. The lines to the left diverge to the High level Bridge and the area now occupied by the car park were once bay platforms at the station. (PJR 05/97)

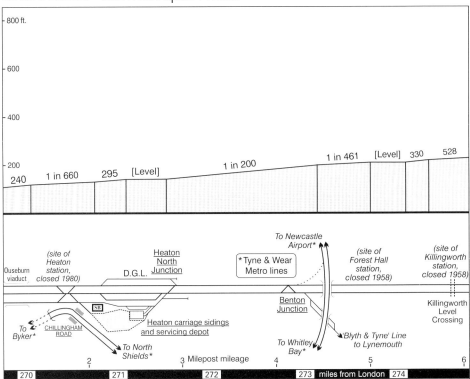

800 ft.

600

400

200

240   1 in 660   295   [Level]   1 in 200   1 in 461   [Level]   330   528

(site of Heaton station, closed 1980)   Ouseburn viaduct

Heaton North Junction   D.G.L.

*Tyne & Wear Metro lines

To Newcastle Airport*

(site of Forest Hall station, closed 1958)

(site of Killingworth station, closed 1958)

SB

Heaton carriage sidings and servicing depot

To Byker*   CHILLINGHAM ROAD

To North Shields*

Benton Junction

To Whitley Bay*

'Blyth & Tyne' Line to Lynemouth

Killingworth Level Crossing

2   3 Milepost mileage   4   5   6

270   271   272   273   miles from London   274

**HEATON** : The Tyne & Wear metro system is an integral part of the transport system in around the City of Newcastle and an example of a metro train (No. 4043) is seen leaving Chillingham Road station on the light rail system. Behind the unit, the view is dominated by Heaton carriage sidings and servicing depot with the ECML running past to the left. (KS 10/01)

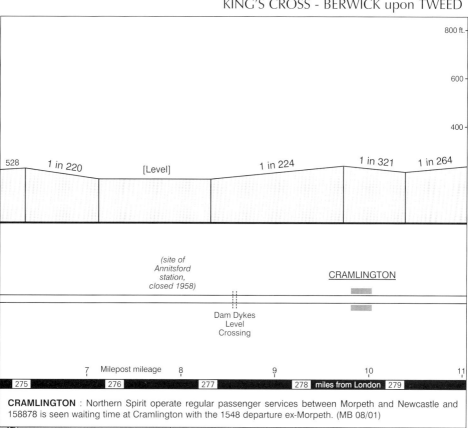

800 ft.

600

400

528    1 in 220    [Level]    1 in 224    1 in 321    1 in 264

*(site of Annitsford station, closed 1958)*

CRAMLINGTON

Dam Dykes
Level
Crossing

7   Milepost mileage   8    9    10    11

275    276    277    278   miles from London   279

**CRAMLINGTON** : Northern Spirit operate regular passenger services between Morpeth and Newcastle and 158878 is seen waiting time at Cramlington with the 1548 departure ex-Morpeth. (MB 08/01)

83

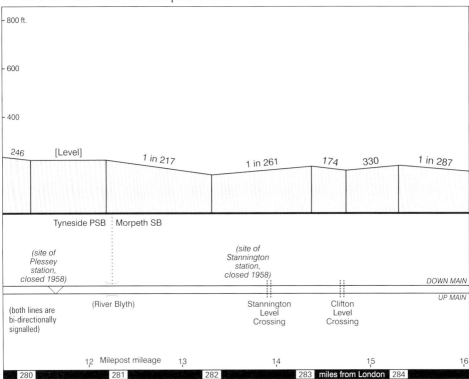

- 800 ft.

- 600

- 400

| 246 | [Level] | 1 in 217 | 1 in 261 | 174 | 330 | 1 in 287 |

Tyneside PSB ┊ Morpeth SB

*(site of Plessey station, closed 1958)*

*(site of Stannington station, closed 1958)*

DOWN MAIN

UP MAIN

(both lines are bi-directionally signalled)

(River Blyth)

Stannington Level Crossing

Clifton Level Crossing

12  Milepost mileage  13         14         15         16

| 280 | 281 | 282 | 283 | miles from London | 284 |

**STANNINGTON** : There are rather surprisingly 31 level crossings between Newcastle and Berwick, of which 27 are controlled by Closed Circuit Television (CCTV). One such example is at Stannington, where a DVT is seen approaching the crossing at the head of 1E16, the 1400 Glasgow Central to King's Cross. Of particular note is the brick building in the picture, which is the base of the former signalbox. (MB 08/01)

84

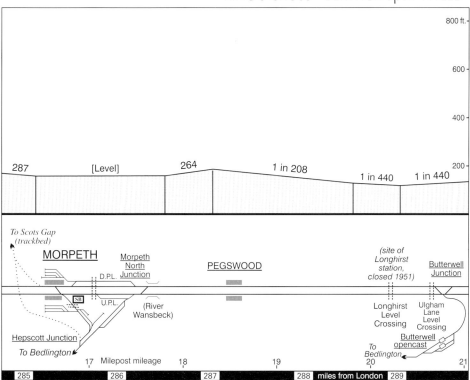

800 ft.

600

400

200

287      [Level]      264      1 in 208      1 in 440      1 in 440

*To Scots Gap (trackbed)*

## MORPETH

Morpeth North Junction

D.PL.

U.PL.

SB

(River Wansbeck)

Hepscott Junction

*To Bedlington*

PEGSWOOD

(site of Longhirst station, closed 1951)

Longhirst Level Crossing

Ulgham Lane Level Crossing

Butterwell Junction

Butterwell opencast

*To Bedlington*

17    Milepost mileage    18        19        20        21

285      286      287      288    miles from London    289

**MORPETH** : Sporting Railfreight International Distribution livery, 90223 passes Morpeth signalbox with 1M51, the Shieldmuir to Willesden mail. The line leading from Morpeth Junction to Bedlington and the 'Blyth & Tyne' is also visible to the right of view. (MB 08/01)

# KING'S CROSS - BERWICK upon TWEED

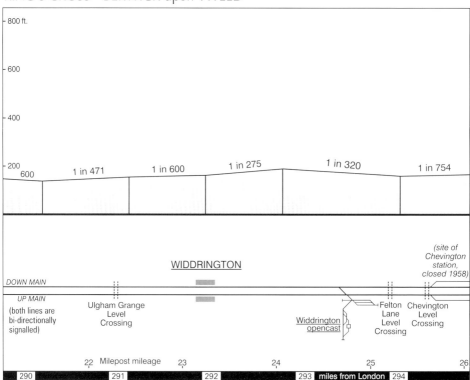

- 800 ft.
- 600
- 400
- 200

| 600 | 1 in 471 | 1 in 600 | 1 in 275 | 1 in 320 | 1 in 754 |

*(site of Chevington station, closed 1958)*

WIDDRINGTON

DOWN MAIN

UP MAIN
(both lines are bi-directionally signalled)

Ulgham Grange Level Crossing

Widdrington opencast

Felton Lane Level Crossing

Chevington Level Crossing

22 Milepost mileage 23 24 25 26

290 291 292 293 **miles from London** 294

**WIDDRINGTON** : As the shadows begin to lengthen, a Class 91 speeds through Widdrington station in charge of 1S01, the 1530 King's Cross to Edinburgh; you will, hopefully, forgive the photographer for failing to obtain the number of the locomotive on this occasion! (MB 08/01)

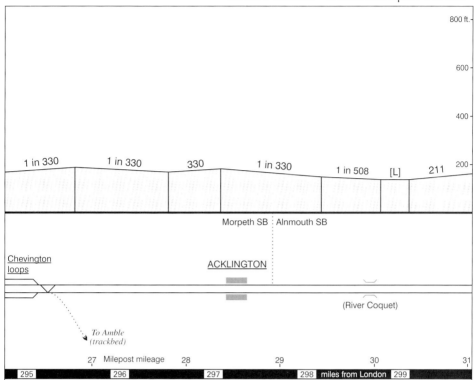

| | | | | | | | |
|---|---|---|---|---|---|---|---|
| 1 in 330 | 1 in 330 | 330 | 1 in 330 | 1 in 508 | [L] | 211 | 200 |

800 ft.
600
400
200

Morpeth SB : Alnmouth SB

Chevington
loops

ACKLINGTON

(River Coquet)

*To Amble*
*(trackbed)*

27 Milepost mileage 28 29 30 31

295 296 297 298 miles from London 299

**ACKLINGTON** : One pleasing aspect of the ECML north of Newcastle is that many old station buildings have been preserved to provide a valuable historical record of North Eastern Railway architecture. At Acklington, an HST lead by 43113 is about to pass the former station building with the first northbound, non-electric, GNER service of the day - 1S11, the 0710 Leeds to Aberdeen. (MB 08/01)

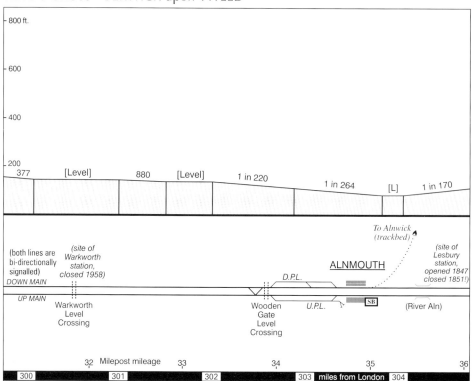

- 800 ft.
- 600
- 400
- 200

| 377 | [Level] | 880 | [Level] | 1 in 220 | 1 in 264 | [L] | 1 in 170 |

To Alnwick
(trackbed)

(both lines are bi-directionally signalled)
DOWN MAIN

(site of Warkworth station, closed 1958)

ALNMOUTH

(site of Lesbury station, opened 1847 closed 1851!)

D.P.L.

UP MAIN

Warkworth Level Crossing

Wooden Gate Level Crossing

U.P.L.

SB

(River Aln)

32   Milepost mileage   33        34        35        36

| 300 | 301 | 302 | 303 | miles from London | 304 |

**ALNMOUTH LOOPS** : Freight activity on the ECML between Newcastle and Edinburgh is sparse to say the least and Anglo-Scottish coal traffic is a welcome bonus. The former coal yard at Alnmouth is to the fore in this view of 66223 proceeding down the main line and past the passenger loops with a rake of MGR empties, forming 6S38, the 1011 Tyne Yard to Falkland Yard. (MB 08/01)

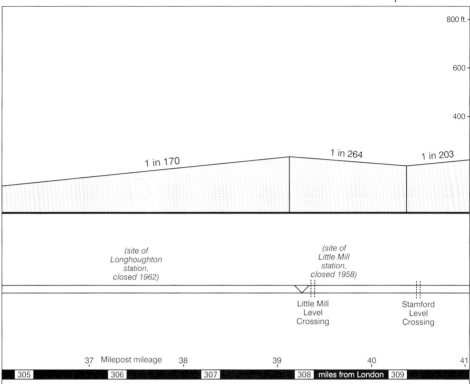

800 ft.

600

400

1 in 170

1 in 264

1 in 203

*(site of
Longhoughton
station,
closed 1962)*

*(site of
Little Mill
station,
closed 1958)*

Little Mill
Level
Crossing

Stamford
Level
Crossing

37  Milepost mileage  38          39          40          41

305      306      307      308  miles from London  309

**ALNMOUTH** : Another MGR service, this time 6U61 the 0726 Chalmerston to Drax, approaches  Alnmouth station headed by 66143, which is dwarfed in comparison to Alnmouth signalbox. This box, which  controls all signals and crossings between Acklington and Chathill, was originally built in 1907 and completely refitted in 1990 with a modern panel to control new bi-directional signalling - note the two signals in view. Some arches of the viaduct which span the River Aln can also be seen to the right of view. (MB 08/01)

# KING'S CROSS - BERWICK upon TWEED

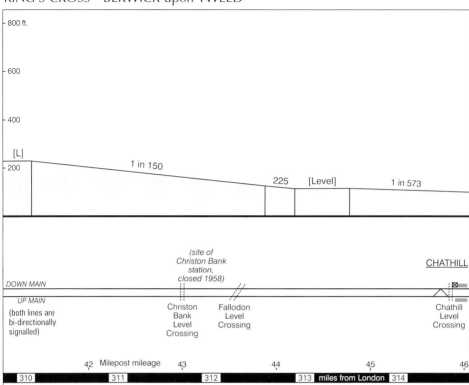

800 ft.

600

400

[L]

200

1 in 150

225    [Level]    1 in 573

(site of
Christon Bank
station,
closed 1958)

CHATHILL

DOWN MAIN

UP MAIN
(both lines are
bi-directionally
signalled)

Christon
Bank
Level
Crossing

Fallodon
Level
Crossing

Chathill
Level
Crossing

42   Milepost mileage   43                44                45                46

310          311          312          313   miles from London   314

**CHATHILL** : No apology is made for including two photographs to illustrate the fine architecture at Chathill. This view shows the station house, which is preserved as a private residence, and the 1873 built signalbox, which now serves as a relay room for signalling equipment and a refuge for permanent way staff. (MB 08/01)

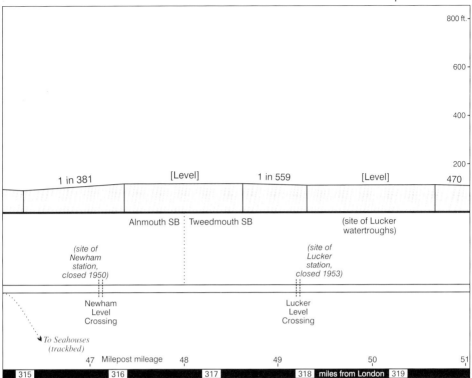

| | | | | |
|---|---|---|---|---|
| 1 in 381 | [Level] | 1 in 559 | [Level] | 470 |

Alnmouth SB : Tweedmouth SB

(site of Lucker
watertroughs)

*(site of
Newham
station,
closed 1950)*

*(site of
Lucker
station,
closed 1953)*

Newham
Level
Crossing

Lucker
Level
Crossing

*To Seahouses
(trackbed)*

47   Milepost mileage   48      49      50      51

315     316     317     318   miles from London   319

**CHATHILL** : The ex-North Eastern Railway waiting room stands proudly on the 'up' platform alongside 'local' milepost 48 as an unidentified DVT enters Chathill station in charge of 1E13, the 1200 Glasgow Central to King's Cross, the "*Flying Scotsman.*" (MB 08/01)

91

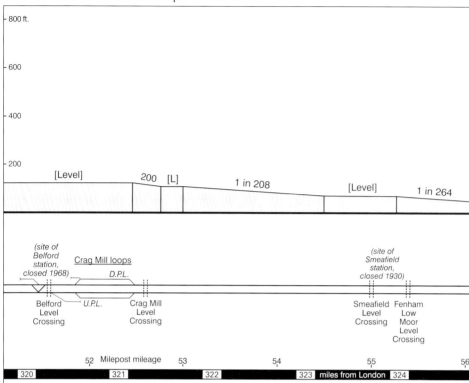

- 800 ft.
- 600
- 400
- 200

[Level]  200  [L]  1 in 208  [Level]  1 in 264

(site of Belford station, closed 1968)  Crag Mill loops  D.P.L.

(site of Smeafield station, closed 1930)

Belford Level Crossing  U.P.L.  Crag Mill Level Crossing  Smeafield Level Crossing  Fenham Low Moor Level Crossing

52  Milepost mileage  53  54  55  56

320  321  322  323  miles from London  324

**BELFORD** : An unidentified HST is seen speeding along the ECML near the village of Belford with 1E12, the 1000 Aberdeen to King's cross "*Northern Lights*" service; the view being dominated by the distinctive grain silos in the background located near Belford Station. (MB 08/01)

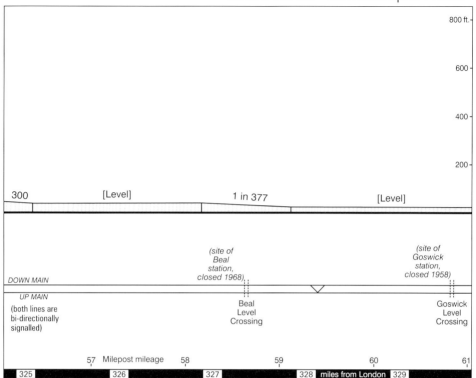

800 ft.

600

400

200

300     [Level]         1 in 377         [Level]

*(site of Beal station, closed 1968),*

*(site of Goswick station, closed 1958)*

DOWN MAIN

UP MAIN

(both lines are bi-directionally signalled)

Beal Level Crossing

Goswick Level Crossing

57   Milepost mileage   58        59        60        61

325       326       327       328   miles from London   329

**BELFORD STATION** : This photograph was taken on the level crossing at Belford Station and, for obvious reasons,there is no train in view. The old station building is on the 'down' side of the line and Crag Mill Loops are located in the middle distance behind the second 25mph sign. The rusted line in the foreground leads to Slater Quarry and a siding for crippled wagons. (MB 08/01)

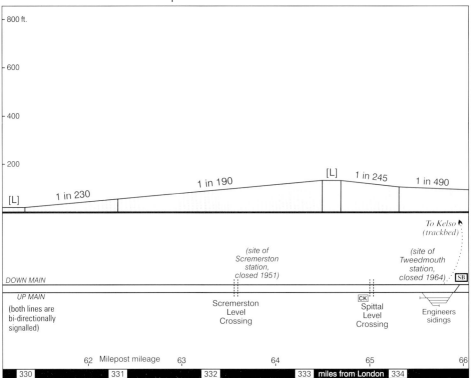

- 800 ft.
- 600
- 400
- 200

[L]    1 in 230    1 in 190    [L]    1 in 245    1 in 490

[L]

*To Kelso* (trackbed)

(site of Scremerston station, closed 1951)

(site of Tweedmouth station, closed 1964)    SB

DOWN MAIN

UP MAIN
(both lines are bi-directionally signalled)

Scremerston Level Crossing

CK
Spittal Level Crossing

Engineers sidings

62    Milepost mileage    63    64    65    66

330    331    332    333    miles from London    334

**SPITTAL** : On a glorious Spring Sunday morning, an HST (43109/43110) passes Spittal with 1E12, the 1150 Aberdeen to King's Cross service, behind which the view is dominated by the town of Berwick upon Tweed and, in particular, the jetty leading to Meadow Haven lighthouse. (PJR 04/95)

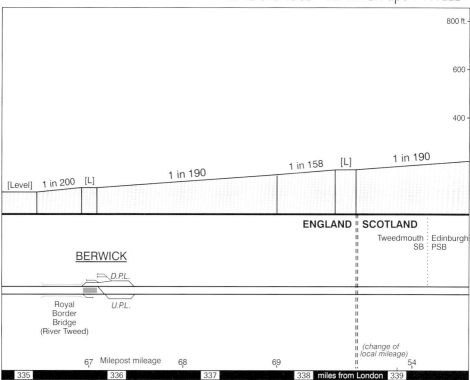

800 ft.

600

400

1 in 190

1 in 158 [L]

1 in 190

[Level] 1 in 200 [L]

ENGLAND ‖ SCOTLAND

Tweedmouth : Edinburgh
SB : PSB

BERWICK

D.P.L.

Royal    U.P.L.
Border
Bridge
(River Tweed)

(change of
local mileage)

67 Milepost mileage    68          69                              54

335          336          337          338 miles from London 339

**ROYAL BORDER BRIDGE** : This magnificent viaduct was so named by Queen Victoria even though it is not actually on the border between England and Scotland. The structure is 28 arches totalling 720 yards in length, carrying the railway 126 feet above the river bed. In this view, a large number of swans can be seen on the river as an unidentified DVT heads across the viaduct with 1E06, the 0930 Edinburgh to King's Cross. (MB 08/01)

95

**BERWICK upon TWEED** : The station at Berwick upon Tweed is an island platform, where 43156 (above) is seen waiting time with 1V49, the 0640 Dundee to Penzance "Cornishman", which along with the "Devon Scot" is the longest cross-country services in the UK. (MB 08/01)

As the late Autumn light begins to fail, 82222 (below) slowly makes its way into Berwick-upon-Tweed with 1E14, the 1400 Edinburgh to King's Cross and past 66136 waiting in the up passenger loop with 6U61, the 0716 Chalmerston to Drax MGR service of power station coal. (MB 12/01)

**Gallery**

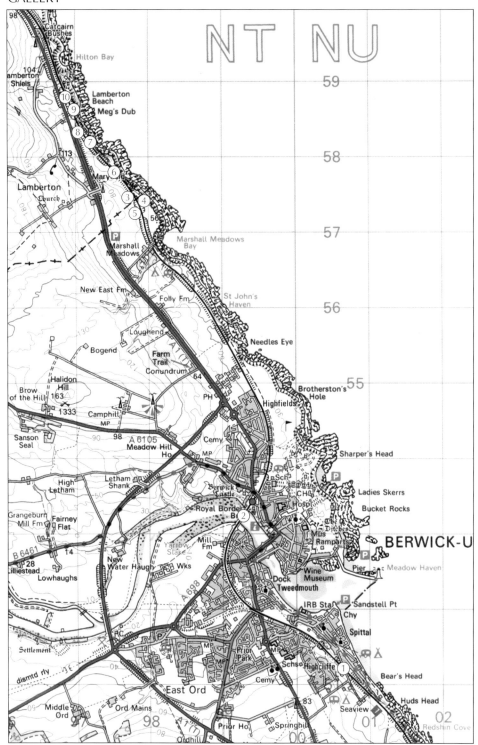

① **SPITTAL** : Looking across the cornfield to the ECML and the River Tweed estuary beyond, we see 86208 *City of Chester* heading the "Capitals Mail" (1E24, 1430 Glasgow Central to King's Cross) away from Berwick-upon-Tweed at Spittal. At the time of writing, this particular train was re-routed to run via Beattock and Hexham before joining up with the ECML again at Newcastle. (PJR 08/96)

② **ROYAL BORDER BRIDGE** : The ECML is blessed with some fine viaducts, notably at Welwyn and Durham, but the one which crosses the River Tweed at Berwick is undoubtedly the most splendid of all. Here, an unidentified Class 91 + Mark 4 set makes its way across the viaduct with 1E05, the 0800 Glasgow Central to King's Cross service. (PJR 02/98)

③ **ANGLO-SCOTTISH BORDER** : The ECML passes from England into Scotland at Marshall Meadows, just over 3 miles north of Berwick, and is illustrated here with two views of the same location to show how different focal lengths provide a contrast. A panoramic view shows off the rugged coastline to good effect as 43096/43111 (above) cross the border with 1E10, the 0755 "Highland Chieftain" service from Inverness to King's Cross. The actual border sign is (out of view) behind the eigth vehicle of the train. (MB 12/01)

④ Meanwhile, a closer view sees 66167 (below) passing Marshall Meadows with a rake of loaded, 'hooded', MGR hoppers forming 6E03, the 0745 Falkland Yard to Doncaster. (MB 12/01)

(5) **ANGLO-SCOTTISH BORDER SIGN** : This decorative sign once again stands proudly by the side of the main line, clearly stating its purpose, although the days of 'British Railways' have long gone. The sign was actually renovated  in 1999 after it had fallen from it's metal frame due to rotten wood being completely impregnated with water. This was, along with the two pictures on the previous page, photographed with the consent of the local farmer. (MB 12/01)

(6) **MARSHALL MEADOWS** : 'Up for the cup' - well, that's what Newcastle United had hoped for in the 1999 FA Cup Final! The empty SRPS coaching stock is seen at Marshall Meadows being hauled by 47766 *Respected* forming 5Z36, B'oness to Tyne Yard, in readiness to take Newcastle football supporters to Wembely the following day. (PJR 05/99)

(7) **LAMBERTON** : The stretch of line where the ECML skirts the North Sea at Lamberton is arguably one of the most scenic in the UK, affording passengers and photographers slplendid views of the Berwickshire coastline. Sporting GNER's blue and red stripe corporate livery, 91020 (above) heads a rake of InterCity liveried coaches on 1S28, the 1300 King's Cross to Edinburgh. (PJR 06/97)

(8) The former Loadhaul black and orange is a striking livery as can be seen on 60038 (below) as it makes its way southwards hauling 6E30, the Dalzell to Lackenby steel empties at Lamberton. (PJR 05/99)

⑨ **LAMBERTON** : The 'up' postal, 1M51,1522 Shieldmuir to Willesden, makes a colourful sight for the photographer as 90038 (above) speeds downhill at Lamberton; note the bi-directional signals. (PJR 07/00)

⑩ Heading in the opposite direction, 37294 (below) heads 6S54, the Byth to Fort William 'Alumina' tanks through gently sweeping curves above the clifftops at Lamberton. Alas, this service is no longer booked for a 'tractor' and is now the preserve of the ubiquitous 'shed' - aka Class 66! (PJR 08/96)

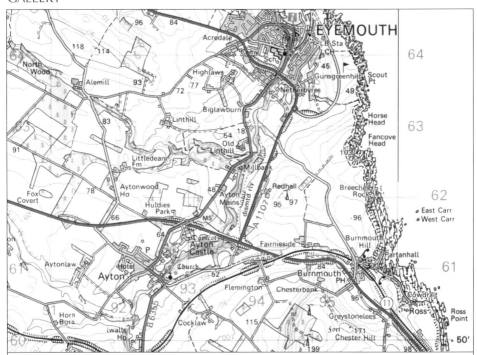

(11) **BURNMOUTH** : By the side of the A1 road, just south of Burnmouth, is a convenient point from which to photograph trains. Here, the line runs along the cliffs and when the biting wind comes in off the North Sea one is reminded that there is nothing between this coast and the North Pole! Looking down from the road and across the fields, we see an HST on 1E08, the 0755 Aberdeen to King's Cross. (MB 12/01)

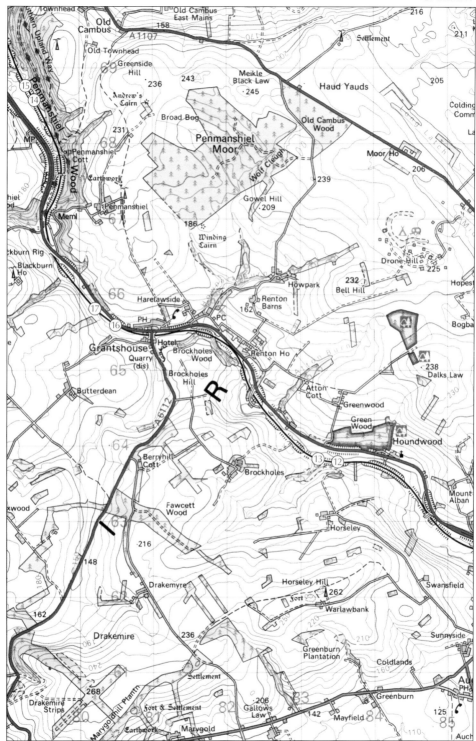

⑫ **HOUNDWOOD** : The quaint village church at Houndwood can be seen behind the train as privately owned Deltic, D9000 *Royal Scots Grey (above),* leaves a plume of smoke in its wake while working the return leg of a Springburn to Tweedmouth test run; 47757 *Restitution* is marshalled inside 'just in case!' (BA 11/96)

⑬ Looking in the opposite direction, the fields of corn have already been harvested as an HST (below) sweeps round the curve at Houndwood with 1E10, the 0755 "Highland Chieftain" service from Inverness to King's Cross; the power cars are 43106 leading with 43113 at the rear. (PJR 09/99)

(14) **PENMANSHIEL** : The ECML passes through the beautiful Penmanshiel Wood valley and is a complete contrast to the scenery we have observed so far in the 'Gallery'. With the Gorse in full bloom, a pair of Class 37s, Nos. 37229+37691 (above) shatter the peace and tranquility as they work hard against the grade on the climb to Grantshouse with 7Z85, the 0825 Redcar Ore Terminal to Millerhill MGR coal train. (PJR 05/93)

(15) The "Royal Scotsman" is a luxurious (and expensive!) charter train, which makes regular 2 & 4-night tours of Scotland from Edinburgh using a set of uniquely liveried coaches. On this occasion, the train is seen away from its normal schedule at Penmanshiel, hauled by dedicated locomotive 37428 (below), heading into England with 1E37, the 1408 Edinburgh to York. (PJR 09/98)

# GALLERY

16 **GRANTSHOUSE** : This delightful picture portrays 6S71, the Thrislington to Inverurie loaded Lime box wagons, headed by 37697 (above), near Grantshouse, where the ECML is very sinuous. Unfortunately, this train no longer runs and Lime is conveyed to Aberdeen on an overnight 'Enterprise' service. (PJR 08/94)

17 The hightest point on the ECML between London King's Cross and Edinburgh Waverley is 400ft. above sea level at Grantshouse. The summit is where the passenger loops are situated, which can be seen in this view of the 'up' "Flying Scotsman" (below) passing the loops on a fine Spring day. (IL 04/01)

**Berwick-upon-Tweed
to
Carstairs**

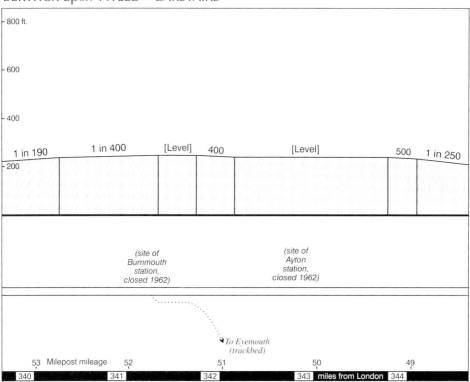

800 ft.

600

400

1 in 190    1 in 400    [Level]    400    [Level]    500    1 in 250

200

(site of
Burnmouth
station,
closed 1962)

(site of
Ayton
station,
closed 1962)

*To Eyemouth*
*(trackbed)*

53   Milepost mileage    52      51      50      49

340     341     342     343   miles from London   344

**HORNBURN** : Sporting BR Civil Engineers/Transrail livery, 37232 *The institution of Railway Signal Engineers* is seen at Hornburn, near Ayton, with 6S54, the Blyth to Fort William Alcan Alumina tanks. Unfortunately, this train is now the preserve of the ubiquitous class 66! (PJR 06/96)

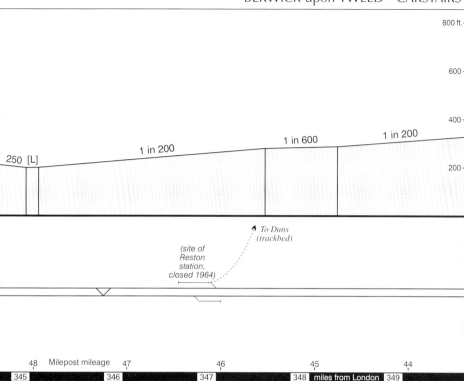

800 ft.

600

400

1 in 200

1 in 600

1 in 200

1 in 200

250 [L]

200

↑ *To Duns*
*(trackbed)*

*(site of*
*Reston*
*station,*
*closed 1964)*

| 48 | Milepost mileage | 47 | | 46 | | 45 | | 44 |
|---|---|---|---|---|---|---|---|---|
| 345 | | | 346 | | 347 | | 348 | miles from London | 349 |

**HOUNDWOOD** : (see overleaf) There are 350 miles to go before the end of the ECML is reached at London King's Cross as the sign at Houndwood clearly indicates. Passing the spot, 60093 *Jack Stirk* heads 6E26, the 1408 Millerhill to Drax loaded MGR containing coal from Ravenstruther, near Carstairs. (PJR 10/98)

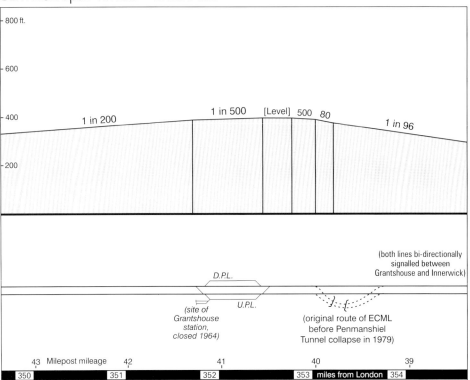

- 800 ft.

- 600

- 400        1 in 200        1 in 500    [Level]  500   80        1 in 96

- 200

(both lines bi-directionally
signalled between
Grantshouse and Innerwick)

D.P.L.

U.P.L.

(site of
Grantshouse
station,
closed 1964)

(original route of ECML
before Penmanshiel
Tunnel collapse in 1979)

43   Milepost mileage    42              41              40              39

350              351            352            353   miles from London   354

**GRANTSHOUSE** : This view, taken from the hillside to the west of the line, shows 66030 running past the passenger loops in charge of 6S38, the 1045 Tyne yard to Falkland yard MGR empties. The village of Grantshouse can be seen in the background behind the train. (IL 04/01)

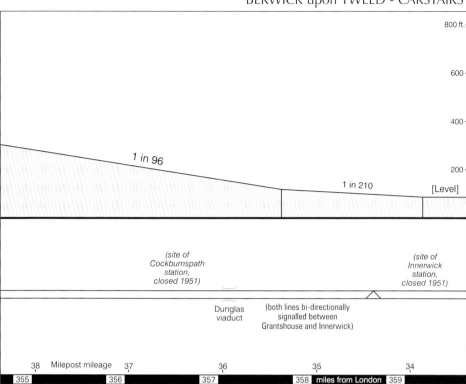

800 ft.

600

400

1 in 96

200

1 in 210

[Level]

(site of
Cockburnspath
station,
closed 1951)

(site of
Innerwick
station,
closed 1951)

Dunglas
viaduct

(both lines bi-directionally
signalled between
Grantshouse and Innerwick)

38    Milepost mileage    37                    36              35              34

355          356          357          358  miles from London  359

**INNERWICK** : As a pleasing break from GNER/EWS train services on this stretch of the main line, this view shows the nuclear power station situated on the coast at Torness (see dieagram overleaf) and 7M30, the Torness to Carlisle nuclear flasks behind 20906/20904. On leaving Torness, the train must first travel to Grantshouse 'up' loop to run round before retracing its steps to  Edinburgh. (IL 04/01)

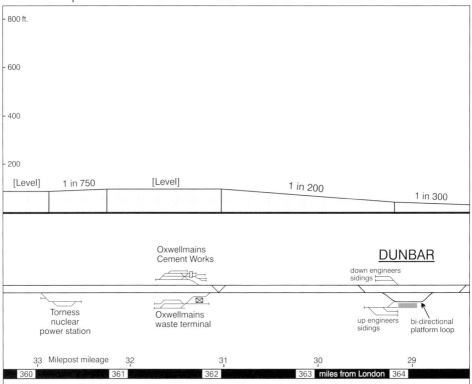

- 800 ft.

- 600

- 400

- 200

[Level]    1 in 750    [Level]    1 in 200    1 in 300

Oxwellmains
Cement Works

**DUNBAR**

down engineers
sidings

Torness
nuclear
power station

Oxwellmains
waste terminal

up engineers
sidings

bi-directional
platform loop

33   Milepost mileage   32    31    30    29

360    361    362    363   miles from London   364

**DUNBAR** : This is one of only two stations within Scotland not served by Scotrail and very few trains call here. The station has a narrow platform - single track/single platform and is effectively a loop off the main line with a crossover at each end. This photograph shows the single line platform, at which DVT 82201 awaits to depart with 1E14, the 1400 Edinburgh Waverley to King's Cross. (IL 04/01)

800 ft.

600

400

200

[L]       1 in 360                [Level]        1 in 600        [L]    1 in 300

(Stenton)

28    Milepost mileage    27              26              25              24

365          366          367          368  miles from London  369

**NORTH BELTON:** The section of line between Dunbar and East Linton runs through a rural agricultural area with no significant landmarks. To the west of North Belton, the line parallels the A1 road and near Hedderwick farm, 43117 (43111 at the rear) heads towards the Scottish capital with 1S20, the 1030 King's Cross to Aberdeen *"Northern Lights"* service. (IL 04/01)

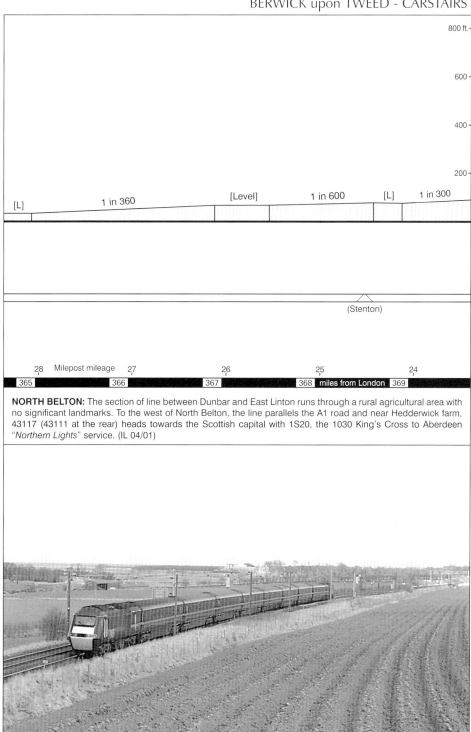

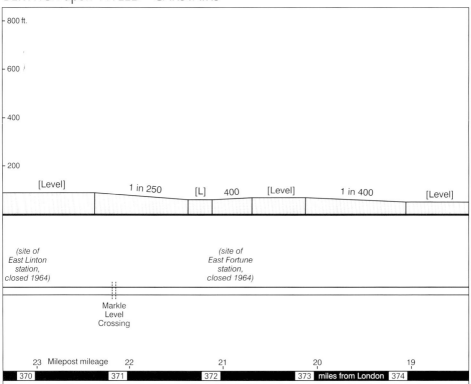

- 800 ft.

- 600

- 400

- 200

[Level]     1 in 250     [L]    400    [Level]     1 in 400     [Level]

*(site of East Linton station, closed 1964)*

*(site of East Fortune station, closed 1964)*

Markle
Level
Crossing

23   Milepost mileage   22           21            20           19

370         371        372      373   **miles from London**   374

**DREM LOOPS** : This view shows the passenger loops just south of Drem station, where 60097 *Pillar passes* with a rake of MGR empties; the train being 6S35, the 0935 Tyne Yard to Ravenstruther. ( IL 04/99)

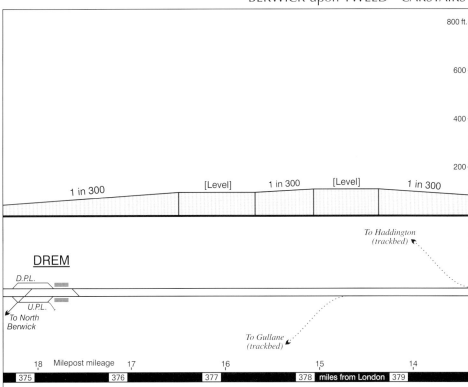

800 ft.-

600 -

400 -

200 -

1 in 300    [Level]    1 in 300    [Level]    1 in 300

*To Haddington*
*(trackbed)*

DREM

D.P.L.

U.P.L.
*To North*
*Berwick*

*To Gullane*
*(trackbed)*

18    Milepost mileage    17    16    15    14

375    376    377    378  miles from London  379

**DREM** : A four-car '305' unit (No. 305501) pauses at Drem with the 1037 Edinburgh Waverley to North Berwick service. The train will gain access to the North Berwick branch from the ECML via the 'up' passenger loop, half a mile to the south of the station. (IL 04/99)

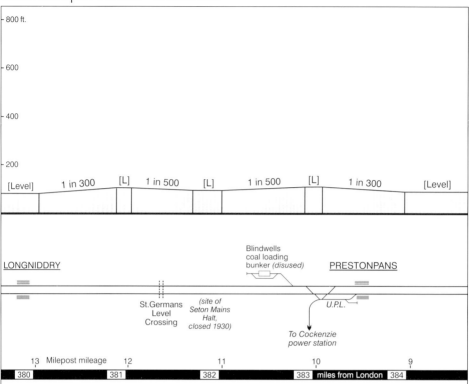

- 800 ft.

- 600

- 400

- 200

[Level] | 1 in 300 | [L] | 1 in 500 | [L] | 1 in 500 | [L] | 1 in 300 | [Level]

LONGNIDDRY

Blindwells
coal loading
bunker *(disused)*

PRESTONPANS

St.Germans
Level
Crossing

*(site of
Seton Mains
Halt,
closed 1930)*

U.P.L.

To Cockenzie
power station

13  Milepost mileage  12          11          10          9

380          381          382          383  miles from London  384

**BLINDWELLS** : The line leading to Blindwells Opencast Disposal Site is in the foreground as 60047 passes by with 6D38, the Oxwellmains to Viewpark loaded cement tanks. The loading bunker can be seen to the right of the picture and the Firth of Forth in the background. (PJR 03/97)

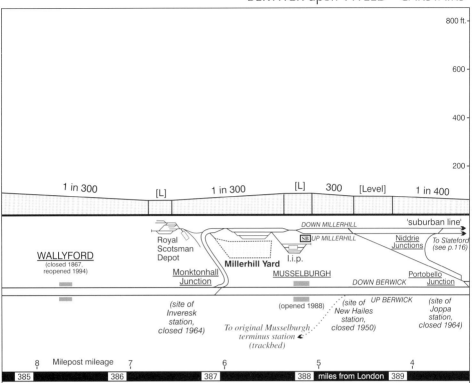

800 ft.

600

400

200

1 in 300    [L]    1 in 300    [L]    300    [Level]    1 in 400

DOWN MILLERHILL    'suburban line'

Royal Scotsman Depot    UP MILLERHILL    SB    Niddrie Junctions    To Slateford (see p.116)

**WALLYFORD**
(closed 1867, reopened 1994)

Monktonhall Junction    **Millerhill Yard**    l.i.p.

MUSSELBURGH    Portobello Junction

DOWN BERWICK

(site of Inveresk station, closed 1964)    (opened 1988)    UP BERWICK    (site of Joppa station, closed 1964)

(site of New Hailes station, closed 1950)

To original Musselburgh terminus station (trackbed)

8    Milepost mileage    7    6    5    4

385    386    387    388    miles from London    389

**PORTOBELLO** : There is plenty of interest in this view as an HST approaches Portobello Junction with 1E10, the 0755 Inverness to King's Cross *"Highland Chieftain."* From left to right, the sidings at Craigentinny, where a GNER set is stabled, the redundant crane at Portobello freightliner terminal directly behind the HST and the Overhead Line Equipment siding at the far right of view. (IL 05/01)

**PORTOBELLO EAST** : EWS liveried 37405 is seen taking the Millerhill line at Portobello East - a single track line off which come the two sidings in the foreground - this is all that remains of what was once the start of the Waverley route to Carlisle. The ECML can be seen snaking away to the left of the class 37 locomotive, which had come from Powderhall after working the Edinburgh 'Binliner.' (IL 05/01)

**MILLERHILL** : Although situated off the ECML, a photograph of Millerhill is justified as it is the main yard for Anglo-Scottish freight traffic using the ECML, especially the many MGR coal trains that are staged here. Looking towards the yard itself, a pair of 37s can be seen stabled as 60021 stops to wait for the signal to let it into the yard with 6E30, the Dalzell to lackenby steel empties. (IL 05/01)

**EDINBURGH WAVERLEY** : Photographed from above Calton Tunnel, a DVT (above) leads a set of Mark 4's +91 out of Waverley station with 1E09, the 1000 Glasgow Central to King's Cross. The track layout at the eastern end of the station is clearly visible and the Edinburgh skyline provides an impressive backdrop. (IL 05/01)

This view of the track layout at the west of Waverley station has been taken from over the mouth of Mound Tunnels and 170408 (below) is seen leaving for Glasgow Queen Street with the 1230 departure from Waverley. Meanwhile, a GNER HST is about to leave platform 19 on the 1230 departure for King's Cross and over in platform 11, a class 91 and Mk. 4 set has just arrived from Craigentinny to work the 1300 service to the English Capital. Another class 170/4 unit is in platform 16 prior to leaving at 1240 for Aberdeen. (IL 05/00)

# BERWICK upon TWEED - CARSTAIRS

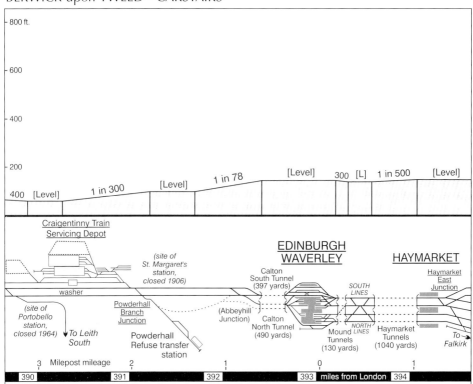

- 800 ft.
- 600
- 400
- 200

1 in 78    [Level]    300   [L]   1 in 500    [Level]

400   [Level]    1 in 300    [Level]

Craigentinny Train
Servicing Depot

(site of
St. Margaret's
station,
closed 1906)

washer

(site of
Portobello
station,
closed 1964)

To Leith
South

Powderhall
Branch
Junction

Powderhall
Refuse transfer
station

(Abbeyhill
Junction)

## EDINBURGH WAVERLEY

Calton
South Tunnel
(397 yards)

Calton
North Tunnel
(490 yards)

Mound
Tunnels
(130 yards)

SOUTH
LINES

NORTH
LINES

## HAYMARKET

Haymarket
East
Junction

Haymarket
Tunnels
(1040 yards)

To
Falkirk

3   Milepost mileage   2    1    0    1

390    391    392    393   miles from London   394

**HAYMARKET** : Looking down the island platform towards Haymarket Tunnels, a Virgin HST set, 43080 leading/43079 rear, arrives at Haymarket station with 1V57, the 0910 Aberdeen to Plymouth "*Devon Scot*", which along with the "*Cornishman*" (see page 96) are the longest passenger services in the UK. (IL 05/00)

122

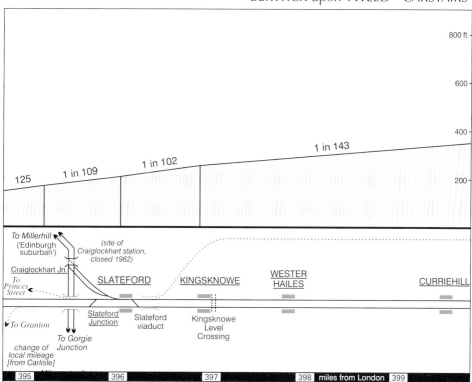

800 ft.

600

400

1 in 143

1 in 102

1 in 109

125

200

To Millerhill
('Edinburgh
suburban')

(site of
Craiglockhart station,
closed 1962)

Craiglockhart Jn
To
Princes
Street

SLATEFORD    KINGSKNOWE    WESTER
HAILES                              CURRIEHILL

To Granton

Slateford
Junction

Slateford
viaduct

Kingsknowe
Level
Crossing

change of    To Gorgie
local mileage  Junction
[from Carlisle]

| 395 | 396 | 397 | 398 | miles from London | 399 |

**SLATEFORD** : The Winter sun is so low in the sky that most of the arches of Slateford viaduct remain in shade as 37520 heads across the viaduct with a ballast train from Carstairs to Millerhill. (BA 02/00)

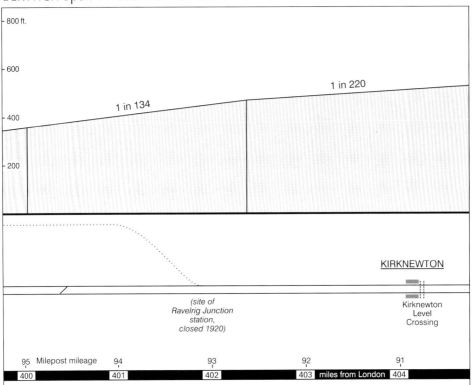

- 800 ft.

- 600

1 in 220

1 in 134

- 400

- 200

KIRKNEWTON

*(site of Ravelrig Junction station, closed 1920)*

Kirknewton Level Crossing

95  Milepost mileage  94          93          92          91
400                   401         402         403 miles from London 404

**KIRKNEWTON** : Substituting for a failed 158 unit, Fragonset-liveried 47705 *Guy Fawkes* top 'n' tails 47711 *County of Hertfordshire* on a rake of four Mk.2 air-conditioned coaches over the level crossing at the west end of Kirknewton station on the 0556 Manchester Airport to Edinburgh service. (IL 11/99)

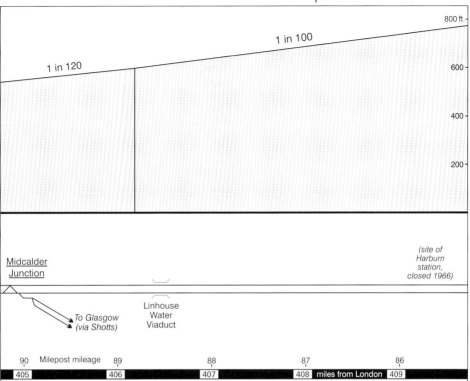

800 ft.

1 in 100

1 in 120

600

400

200

Midcalder
Junction

*(site of Harburn station, closed 1966)*

Linhouse
Water
Viaduct

*To Glasgow
(via Shotts)*

| 90 | Milepost mileage | 89 | | 88 | | 87 | | 86 |

| 405 | | 406 | | 407 | | 408 | miles from London | 409 |

**MIDCALDER** : This was the final straw (photograph) to complete the pictorial 5-mile sections of the route and shows 91017 *City of Leeds* in charge of 1S14, the 0800  King's cross to Glasgow Central "*Scottish Pullman*" emerging from a cutting at Midcalder. Midcalder Junction is where the main line departs for Glasgow via Shotts and is situated out of sight to the right of the cutting. (MB 12/01)

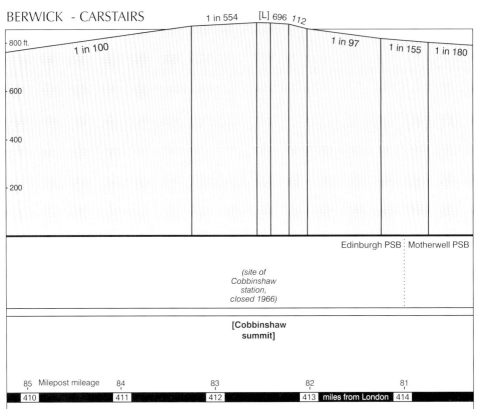

1 in 554    [L] 696  112

800 ft.

1 in 100

1 in 97    1 in 155    1 in 180

600

400

200

Edinburgh PSB : Motherwell PSB

(site of
Cobbinshaw
station,
closed 1966)

[Cobbinshaw
summit]

85   Milepost mileage    84      83      82      81

410       411       412       413   miles from London   414

**COBBINSHAW SUMMIT** : The climb from Edinburgh to Cobbinshaw summit can still pose problems for modern motive power if rail conditions are poor. At the summit, an unidentified Class 86 locomotive sweeps past Cobbinshaw reservoir in charge of 1M67, the 1755 (Sun) Edinburgh to Manchester Piccadilly. (RR 08/01)

126

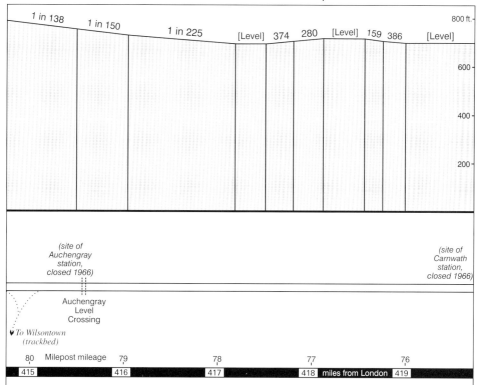

1 in 138    1 in 150    1 in 225    [Level]   374   280   [Level]   159   386   [Level]    800 ft.

600
400
200

*(site of Auchengray station, closed 1966)*

*(site of Carnwath station, closed 1966)*

Auchengray Level Crossing

*To Wilsontown (trackbed)*

80   Milepost mileage   79     78     77     76

415    416    417    418   miles from London   419

**AUCHENGRAY** : The area around Auchengray is very photogenic as evidenced by this superb composition of 56114, nicely framed between two trees, heading towards Cobbinshaw Summit with a loaded MGR working from Ravenstruther to Cockenzie power station. (BA 11/95)

127

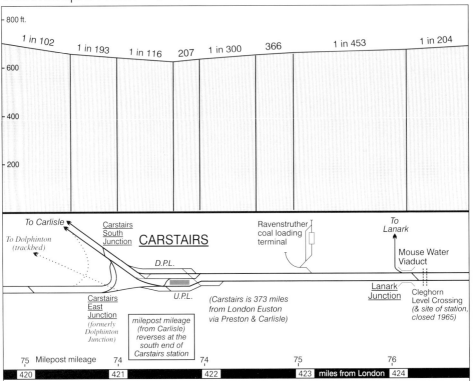

800 ft.

1 in 102 | 1 in 193 | 1 in 116 | 207 | 1 in 300 | 366 | 1 in 453 | 1 in 204

600

400

200

To Carlisle

To Dolphinton *(trackbed)*

Carstairs South Junction

**CARSTAIRS**

*D.P.L.*

Carstairs East Junction *(formerly Dolphinton Junction)*

*U.P.L.*

*milepost mileage (from Carlisle) reverses at the south end of Carstairs station*

*(Carstairs is 373 miles from London Euston via Preston & Carlisle)*

Ravenstruther coal loading terminal

To Lanark

Mouse Water Viaduct

Lanark Junction

Cleghorn Level Crossing (& site of station, closed 1965)

75   Milepost mileage   74    74    75    76

420    421    422    423   miles from London   424

**CARSTAIRS** : A two-car 158 unit (158751) is seen at Carstairs East Junction heading for Edinburgh on the 0558 Manchester Airport to Edinburgh Waverley after its stop at Carstairs. The use of a telephoto lens fore-shortens the view, but accentuates the lines of the West Coast main Line in the foreground. Alas, after leaving London King's Cross and travelling more than 400 miles, we reach the end of our journey in volume 3 of Line By Line featuring the East Coast Main Line. (IL 05/01)

The
Hertford
Loop

# HERTFORD LOOP

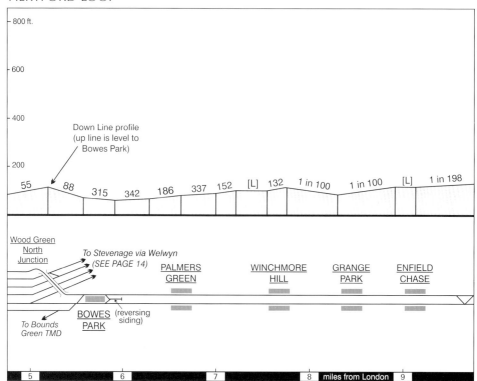

800 ft.

600

400

Down Line profile
(up line is level to
Bowes Park)

200

55  88  315  342  186  337  152  [L]  132  1 in 100  1 in 100  [L]  1 in 198

Wood Green
North
Junction

To Stevenage via Welwyn
(SEE PAGE 14)

PALMERS
GREEN

WINCHMORE
HILL

GRANGE
PARK

ENFIELD
CHASE

BOWES (reversing
PARK   siding)

To Bounds
Green TMD

5   6   7   8   miles from London   9

**WINCHMORE HILL** : Mainline passenger services are frequently diverted on a Sunday via the Hertford Loop to allow engineering work to be carried out on the ECML between Alexandra Palace and Stevenage. One such service is the 1100 King's Cross to Aberdeen, seen passing through Winchmore Hill, where 43117 is the leading power car of the HST train set. (BB 06/01)

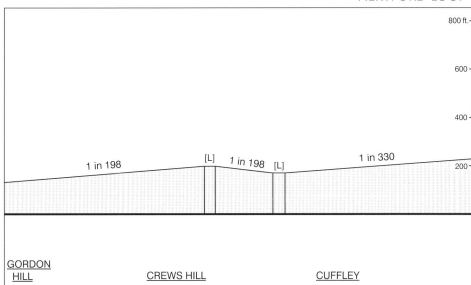

800 ft.

600

400

1 in 198    [L]   *1 in 198*   [L]      1 in 330    200

GORDON
HILL

CREWS HILL

CUFFLEY

10      11      12      13   miles from London   14

**GORDON HILL** : A small number of passengers await the arrival of 317306 with a Hertford North to King's Cross service; note the old footbridge linking the platforms in the background. (BB 06/01)

131

# HERTFORD LOOP

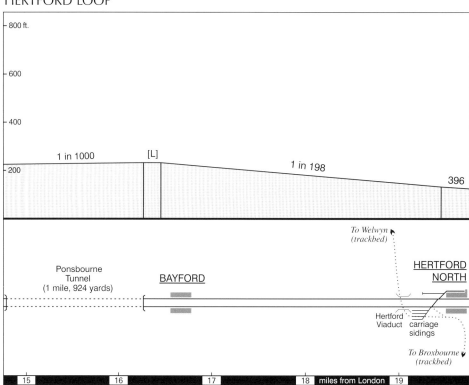

800 ft.

600

400

1 in 1000    [L]

200            *1 in 198*

396

*To Welwyn*
*(trackbed)*

Ponsbourne
Tunnel
(1 mile, 924 yards)

**BAYFORD**

HERTFORD
NORTH

Hertford
Viaduct   carriage
sidings

*To Broxbourne*
*(trackbed)*

| 15 | 16 | 17 | 18 | miles from London | 19 |

**HERTFORD NORTH** : Another diverted mainline service, 1Sxx, the 1400 King's Cross to Edinburgh is seen passing through Hertford North, as 317335 waits to depart for King's Cross. (BB 06/01)

132

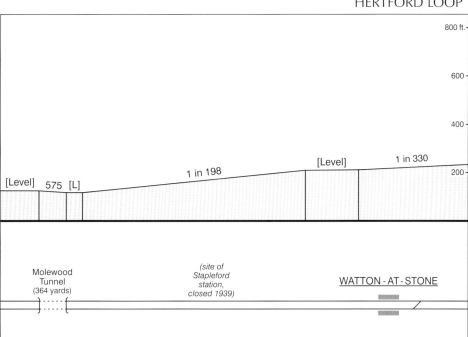

800 ft.

600

400

[Level]          1 in 330
                                                    200
                1 in 198

[Level]   575  [L]

Molewood                      (site of
Tunnel                        Stapleford              WATTON‑AT‑STONE
(364 yards)                   station,
                              closed 1939)

20        21        22        23  miles from London  24

**WATTON** : A Networker Class 365 EMU, 365522, passes through Watton station at speed with an up working, still sporting the old Network South‑East livery. (BB 06/01)

133

# HERTFORD LOOP

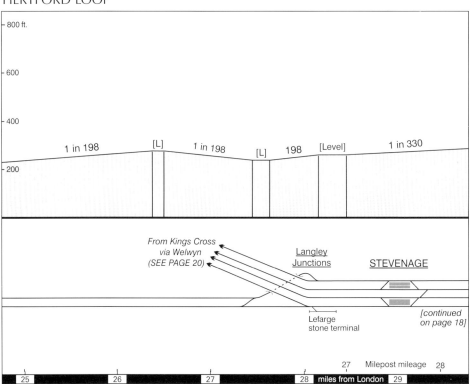

- 800 ft.

- 600

- 400

1 in 198     [L]     1 in 198     [L]    198    [Level]     1 in 330

- 200

From Kings Cross
via Welwyn
(SEE PAGE 20)

Langley
Junctions

STEVENAGE

Lefarge
stone terminal

[continued
on page 18]

27    Milepost mileage    28

| 25 | 26 | 27 | 28 | miles from London | 29 |

**LANGLEY JUNCTION** : In the background, the ECML can be seen in this view of 313060 joining the Hertford Loop with the 1248 Letchworth to Moorgate service. (MR 03/00)

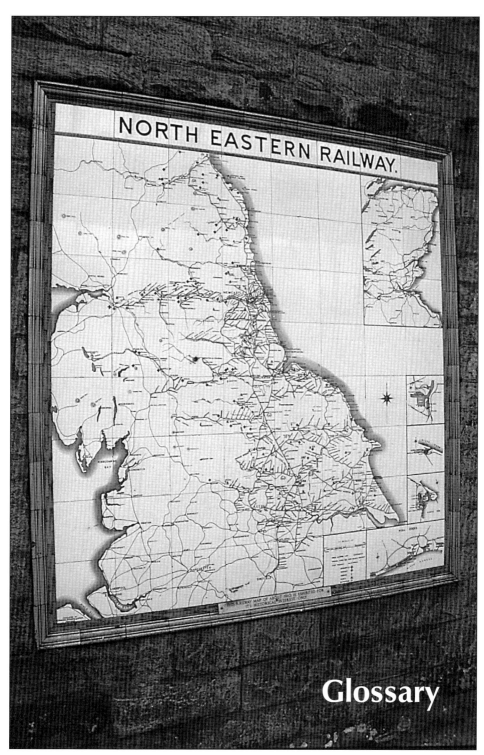

**Glossary**

# Miles and Chains

These tables set out the mileage for the East Coast Main Line in the down direction from London King's Cross to Edinburgh Waverley, thence to Carstairs to link up with the West Coast Main Line. The 'Hertford Loop' is also included.

Cumulative Mileage is given in Miles and Chains plus the Local Mileage when local mileposts replace the cumulative ones besides the running lines. Every station, junction and tunnel is listed under Location; stations are highlighted in bold typeface along with a note of the Page Number for reference.

## 1. LONDON KING'S CROSS - EDINBURGH WAVERLEY - CARSTAIRS

| Cumulative Mileage (M. Chs.) | Local Mileage (M. Chs.) | Location | Page Number |
|---|---|---|---|
| 0. 00 | | **LONDON KINGS CROSS** | 12 |
| 0. 22 | | *Gasworks Tunnels (south portals)* | |
| 0. 46 | | *Gasworks Tunnels (north portals)* | |
| 0. 64 | | *Freight terminal Junction* | |
| 0. 65 | | *Copenhagen Tunnels (south portals)* | |
| 1. 12 | | *Copenhagen Tunnels (south portals)* | |
| **2. 41** | | **Finsbury Park** | 12 |
| 3. 29 | | *Haringay Junction* | |
| **3. 32** | | **Haringay** | 12 |
| 3. 40 | | *Ferme Park South Junction* | |
| 3. 74 | | *Ferme Park North Junction* | |
| **4. 04** | | **Hornsey** | 12 |
| **4. 78** | | **Alexandra Palace** | 14 |
| 4. 68 | | *Wood Green South Junction* | |
| 5. 07 | | *Wood Green North Junction* | |
| 5. 41 | | *Wood Green Tunnels (south portals)* | |
| 5. 73 | | *Wood Green Tunnels (north portals)* | |
| **6. 35** | | **New Southgate** | 14 |
| 7. 42 | | *Barnet Tunnel (south portal)* | |
| 7. 70 | | *Barnet Tunnel (north portal)* | |
| **8. 30** | | **Oakleigh Park** | 14 |
| **9. 12** | | **New Barnet** | 14 |
| 10. 21 | | *Hadley Wood South Tunnels (south portals)* | |
| 10. 39 | | *Hadley Wood South Tunnels (north portals)* | |
| **10. 46** | | **Hadley Wood** | 15 |
| 10. 60 | | *Hadley Wood North Tunnels (south portal)* | |
| 10. 70 | | *Hadley Wood North Tunnels (north portal)* | |
| 11. 25 | | *Potters Bar Tunnels (south portals)* | |
| 12. 00 | | *Potters Bar Tunnels (north portals)* | |
| **12. 57** | | **Potters Bar** | 15 |
| **14. 37** | | **Brookmans Park** | 15 |
| **15. 45** | | **Welham Green** | 16 |

| (M. Ch) | (M. Ch) | Location | Page |
|---|---|---|---|
| 17. 54 | | **Hatfield** | **16** |
| 20. 25 | | **Welwyn Garden City** | **17** |
| 22. 00 | | **Welwyn North** | **17** |
| 22. 11 | | *Welwyn South Tunnel (south portal)* | |
| 22. 31 | | *Welwyn South Tunnel (north portal)* | |
| 22. 44 | | *Welwyn North Tunnel (south portal)* | |
| 23. 12 | | *Welwyn North Tunnel (north portal)* | |
| 25. 03 | | **Knebworth** | **20** |
| 26. 45 | | *Langley Junction (up)* | |
| 26. 59 | | *Langley Junction (down)* | |
| 27. 45 | | **STEVENAGE** | **20** |
| 31. 74 | | **Hitchin** | **22** |
| 32. 11 | | *Cambridge Junction* | |
| 37. 03 | | **Arlesey** | **23** |
| 41. 13 | | **Biggleswade** | **24** |
| 44. 10 | | **Sandy** | **24** |
| 51. 58 | | **St. Neots** | **26** |
| 58. 70 | | **Huntingdon** | **27** |
| 74. 71 | | *Fletton Junction* | |
| 76. 25 | | *Crescent Junction* | |
| 76. 29 | | **PETERBOROUGH** | **31** |
| 79. 34 | | *Werrington Junction* | |
| 81. 56 | | *Helpston Junction* | |
| 100. 07 | | ***Stoke Summit* (345 ft.)** | |
| 100. 39 | | *Stoke Tunnel (south portal)* | |
| 100. 79 | | *Stoke Tunnel (north portal)* | |
| 105. 38 | | **GRANTHAM** | **39** |
| 106. 08 | | *Nottingham Branch Junction* | |
| 107. 65 | | *Peascliffe Tunnel (south portal)* | |
| 108. 29 | | *Peascliffe Tunnel (north portal)* | |
| 109. 56 | | *Barkston South Junction* | |
| 120. 08 | | **NEWARK NORTH GATE** | **43** |
| 120. 51 | | *Newark Crossing South Junction* | |
| 120. 63 | | *Newark Crossing* | |
| 134. 37 | | *Askham Tunnel (south portal)* | |
| 134. 40 | | *Askham Tunnel (north portal)* | |
| 138. 49 | | **RETFORD** | **46** |
| 138. 55 | | *Retford Western Junction* | |
| 149. 28 | | *Pipers Wood Summit* | |
| 152. 00 | | *Loversall Carr Junction* | |
| 116. 44 | | *Black Carr Junction* | |
| 116. 71 | | *Decoy South Junction* | |
| 154. 02 | | *Potteric Carr Junction* | |
| 117. 46 | | *Decoy North Junction* | |
| 155. 28 | | *Sand Bank Junction* | |
| 155. 38 | | *Bridge Junction* | |
| 155. 58 | | *South Yorkshire Junction* | |
| 155. 77 | | **DONCASTER** | **51** |
| 156. 26 | | *Marshgate Junction* | |
| 158. 45 | | *Bentley Colliery South Junction* | |
| 158. 68 | | *Bentley Colliery North Junction* | |
| 160. 16 | | *Shaftholme Junction* | |
| 160. 48 | | *Joan Croft Junction* | |
| 169. 16 | | *Temple Hirst Junction* | |

# GLOSSARY

| (M. Ch) | (M. Ch) | Location | Page |
|---|---|---|---|
| 174. 15 | | *Hambleton South Junction* | |
| 174. 75 | | *Hambleton North Junction* | |
| 182. 79 | | *Colton Junction* | |
| 188. 07 | | *Holgate Junction* | |
| **188. 40** | **0. 00** | **YORK** | 61 |
| 190. 10 | 1. 50 | *Skelton Junction* | |
| **210. 56** | **22. 16** | **THIRSK** | 68 |
| 217. 27 | 28. 67 | *Longlands Junction* | |
| **218. 36** | **29. 76** | **NORTHALLERTON** | 69 |
| 218. 49 | 30. 09 | *High Junction* | |
| 219. 19 | 30. 59 | *Castle Hills Junction* | |
| 232. 21 | 43. 61 | *Darlington South Junction* | |
| **232. 50** | **44. 10** | **DARLINGTON** | 72 |
| 233. 18 | 44. 58 | *Parkgate Junction* | |
| 244. 57 | 56. 17 | *Ferryhill South Junction* | |
| 246. 10 | 57. 50 | *Kelloe Bank Foot Junction* | |
| 247. 31 | 58. 71 | *Tursdale Junction* | |
| **254. 53** | **66. 13** | **DURHAM** | 77 |
| **260. 12** | **71. 72** | **Chester-Le-Street** | 78 |
| 263. 69 | 75. 29 | *Birtley Junction* | |
| 265. 77 | 77. 37 | *Low Fell Junction* | |
| 268. 02 | 79. 42 | *King Edward Bridge South Junction* | |
| 268. 17 | 79. 57 | *King Edward Bridge North Junction* | |
| 268. 45 | 80. 05 | *Newcastle West Junction* | |
| **268. 56** | **80. 16** | **NEWCASTLE CENTRAL** | 79 |
| 268. 70 | 0. 14 | *Newcastle East Junction* | |
| **269. 22** | **0. 46** | **Manors** | 80 |
| 269. 41 | 0. 65 | *Red Barns Tunnel (south portal)* | |
| 269. 46 | 0. 70 | *Red Barns Tunnel (north portal)* | |
| 270. 41 | 1. 65 | *Heaton South Junction* | |
| 272. 42 | 2. 66 | *Heaton North Junction* | |
| 273. 00 | 4. 24 | *Benton Junction* | |
| **278. 50** | **9. 74** | **Cramlington** | 83 |
| **285. 26** | **16. 50** | **Morpeth** | 85 |
| 285. 32 | 16. 56 | *Morpeth Junction* | |
| 286. 02 | 17. 26 | *Morpeth North Junction* | |
| **287. 20** | **18. 44** | **Pegswood** | 85 |
| 289. 39 | 20. 63 | *Butterwell Junction* | |
| **291. 76** | **23. 20** | **Widdrington** | 86 |
| **297. 19** | **28. 43** | **Acklington** | 87 |
| **303. 45** | **34. 69** | **ALNMOUTH** | 88 |
| **314. 57** | **46. 01** | **Chathill** | 90 |
| **335. 56** | **67. 00** | **BERWICK-UPON-TWEED** | 95 |
| **338. 43** | **54. 49** | *ER/ScR Boundary* | |
| **364. 07** | **29. 05** | **Dunbar** | 114 |
| 375. 13 | 17. 79 | *Drem Junction* | |
| **375. 32** | **17. 60** | **Drem** | 117 |
| **379. 74** | **13. 18** | **Longniddry** | 118 |
| **383. 52** | **9. 40** | **Prestonpans** | 118 |
| **385. 37** | **7. 55** | **Wallyford** | 119 |
| 387. 14 | 5. 78 | *Monktonhall Junction* | |
| **387. 78** | **5. 14** | **Musselburgh** | 119 |
| 389. 62 | 3. 30 | *Portobello Junction* | |
| 391. 21 | 1. 71 | *Powderhall Branch Junction* | |

| (M. Ch) | (M. Ch) | Location | Page |
|---|---|---|---|
| 391. 57 | 1. 35 | *St. Margarets Tunnel (east portal)* | |
| 391. 60 | 1. 32 | *St. Margarets Tunnel (west portal)* | |
| 392. 44 | 0. 48 | *Calton Tunnel (east portal)* | |
| 392. 62 | 0. 30 | *Calton Tunnel (west portal)* | |
| **393. 12** | **0. 00** | **EDINBURGH WAVERLEY** | 122 |
| 393. 28 | 0. 16 | *Mound Tunnels (east portals)* | |
| 393. 34 | 0. 22 | *Mound Tunnels (west portals)* | |
| 393. 59 | 0. 47 | *Haymarket Tunnels (east portals)* | |
| 394. 26 | 1. 14 | *Haymarket Tunnels (west portals)* | |
| **394. 31** | **1. 19** | **HAYMARKET** | 122 |
| 394. 36 | 100. 41 | *Haymarket East Junction* | |
| 395. 76 | 99. 01 | *Slateford Junction* | |
| **396. 02** | **98. 75** | **Slateford** | 123 |
| **396. 72** | **98. 05** | **Kingsknowe** | 123 |
| **397. 60** | **97. 17** | **Wester Hailes** | 123 |
| **399. 35** | **95. 42** | **Curriehill** | 123 |
| **404. 07** | **90. 70** | **Kirknewton** | 124 |
| 404. 71 | 90. 06 | *Midcalder Junction* | |
| 412. 32 | 82. 45 | **Cobbinshaw Summit (880 ft.)** | |
| 420. 00 | 74. 77 | *Carstairs East Junction* | |
| **421. 24** | **73. 53** | **CARSTAIRS** | 128 |

## 2. HERTFORD LOOP

| Cumulative Mileage | Local Mileage | Location | Page Number |
|---|---|---|---|
| (M. Ch) | (M. Ch) | | |
| 5. 07 | | *Wood Green North Junction* | |
| 5. 40 | | *Bowes Park Junction* | |
| **5. 55** | | **Bowes park** | 130 |
| **6. 50** | | **Palmers Green** | 130 |
| **7. 63** | | **Winchmore Hill** | 130 |
| **8. 35** | | **Grange Park** | 130 |
| **9. 09** | | **Enfield Chase** | 130 |
| **9. 69** | | **Gordon Hill** | 131 |
| **11. 40** | | **Crews Hill** | 131 |
| **13. 17** | | **Cuffley** | 131 |
| 14. 59 | | *Ponsbourne Tunnel (south portal)* | |
| 16. 21 | | *Ponsbourne Tunnel (north portal)* | |
| **16. 56** | | **Bayford** | 132 |
| **19. 48** | | **HERTFORD NORTH** | 132 |
| 20. 14 | | *Molewood Tunnel (south portal)* | |
| 20. 31 | | *Molewood Tunnel (north portal)* | |
| **23. 72** | | **Watton-At-Stone** | 133 |
| 27. 25 | | *Langley South Junction* | |

# Acknowledgements

The map extracts in the 'Gallery' are kindly reproduced from Landranger 1 : 50 000 scale Ordnance Survey maps by permission of Ordnance Survey on behalf of the Controller of Her Majesty's Stationary Office, © Crown Copyright MC0100028152:

| Sheet Number | Landranger Map Title | Date |
|---|---|---|
| 67 | Duns, Dunbar & Eyemouth | 2001 |
| 75 | Berwick-upon-Tweed | 2000 |

The Photographers who have kindly contributed material for this book are named below along with a note of their initials, which have been used throughout for the purpose of accreditation.

| | | | | | |
|---|---|---|---|---|---|
| Bob Avery | (BA) | Brian Beer | (BB) | Chris Booth | (CB) |
| Martin Buck | (MB) | Nigel Gibbs | (NG) | Ian Lothian | (IL) |
| Brian Morrison | (BM) | John Rudd | (JR) | Mark Rawlinson | (MR) |
| Peter J Robinson | (PJR) | Robin Ralston | (RR) | Ken Short | (KS) |

Brief details of the non-captioned photographs are as follows:

| Page | Location | Description | By |
|---|---|---|---|
| 11 | King's Cross | 3312 : 1X33, 1430 King's Cross - York | BB (10/01) |
| 97 | Penmanshiel | 91017 : 1S23, 1130 King's Cross - Edinburgh | PJR (08/95) |
| 109 | Edinburgh | HST : 1S20, 1030 King's Cross - Aberdeen | MB (08/99) |
| 129 | Hertford North | 82231 : 1E04, 1030 Edinburgh - King's - Cross | BB (06/01) |
| 135 | Morpeth | Tiled wall map of ex-North Eastern Railway network | MB (08/01) |

# Bibliography

| | | |
|---|---|---|
| Railway Track Diagrams (1. Scotland) | : Quail Map Company | ISBN 1-898319-51-0 |
| Railway Track Diagrams (2. England : East) | : Quail Map Company | ISBN 1-898319-29-14 |
| Rail Atlas (GB & Ireland) | : Haynes Publishing | ISBN 0-86093-534-5 |
| Gradient Profiles | : Ian Allan Ltd | ISBN 0-7110-0875-2 |
| East Coast Electrification | : Ian Allan Ltd | ISBN 0-7110-1979-7 |
| Freightmaster* | : Freightmaster Publishing | ISSN 1357-4841 |
| Class One* | : Freightmaster Publishing | ISSN 1465-6973 |

* various editions used for train identification purposes.

Also, the following cab ride videos of the route from Video 125 are highly recommended:

| | |
|---|---|
| The Flying Scotsman : 1 - Kings Cross to York | ISBN 027671-000295 |
| The Flying Scotsman : 2 - York to Edinburgh | ISBN 027671-000301 |